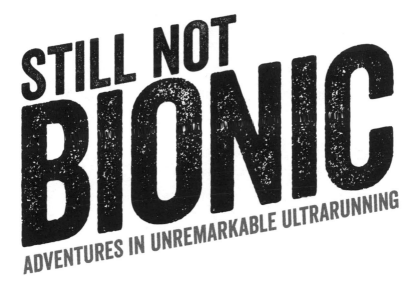

STILL NOT BIONIC

ADVENTURES IN UNREMARKABLE ULTRARUNNING

IRA RAINEY

◆Tangent Books

This edition published 2016 by Tangent Books

Tangent Books
Unit 5.16 Paintworks
Bristol
BS4 3EH
0117 972 0645
www.tangentbooks.co.uk

ISBN 978-1-910089-53-8

Publisher: Richard Jones (richard@tangentbooks.co.uk)
Design: Joe Burt (joe@wildsparkdesign.co.uk)

Cover images © Andrew Rendell / Brandon Griffiths (AWOL Adventure)

A CIP catalogue record for this book is available from the British Library.

Printed using paper from a sustainable source

This book is dedicated to

George

For constantly supporting, nursing and tolerating me

Contents

Foreword

During the summer of 2012, I started training to run my first ultramarathon around my home city of Bristol. I had no prior experience of running ultra distances and didn't know much about how to, so I asked questions, gathered knowledge and embarked on a journey to complete the 45 mile Green Man Ultra. Because it seemed like a good idea at the time I also then ran a further 13.1 miles the next day in the Bath Half Marathon. It was a challenging yet rewarding weekend and, although I achieved what I set out to, it's fair to say not everything turned out as expected.

I wrote about everything that happened in the book *Fat Man to Green Man: From Unfit to Ultramarathon*. It's an honest and frank story of how an average runner such as myself can take on - what looked like at the time - an impossible feat and succeed. The story shows that with the right focus, a positive mindset and by surrounding yourself with the right people, it is possible to accomplish things you previously saw as unattainable.

The book was well-received, far outstripping any humble expectations I had of it. In 2014 it won the silver prize for books at The Running Awards. I was also short-listed for Best New Writer in the British Sports Book Awards the same year. Even more unexpected was the steady stream of positive messages I received from people after publication. Through their ability to relate to my unremarkable normalness, many were motivated by a newfound confidence and inspired to do more with their own running. When I wrote *Fat Man to Green Man*, I could never have imagined how well it would be received nor how it would help others. I also couldn't know how the story I intended to write would itself be rewritten by the uncertainty of life it was in part about.

What I've learnt over the past few years is that running ultramarathons takes a certain state of mind. It requires determination, bloody-mindedness and lots of self-belief. What goes on inside your head is often more important than your actual physical fitness. Some people consider running such distances to be around 50 percent psychological, while other people would argue that that percentage is even higher. If that is the case, what happens when your mental fortitude is eroded or even non-existent to begin with? How does your mental health affect your ability to get out and run - and vice versa? These are all questions I've had to tackle over the last few years and which I touch on in this second book.

My perception of such events is now very different than it was four years ago. After running a dozen ultras along canals, on trails and up and down mountains in only three years it would be impossible for it to not be. Yet I still don't allow it to overwhelm the rest of my life, nor do I take it too seriously. While I train for success, I do it with one eye on the adventure of completing the challenge. Enjoyment is every bit as important as finishing. The ongoing joke among my friends is that any new book I write should be called *Green Man to Fat Man*. While I haven't ballooned back to my pre-ultrarunning girth, the fact I have regained a few pounds over recent years is inescapable. However, it's not something that has put a cap on my capability because I'm not looking to win anything.

Before running my first ultra I read a lot of books on the subject. Although varied, most of them were epic tales that made the challenges within them seem unreachable. Stories featuring runners such as Dean Karnazes, Scott Jurek and Killian Jornet, while fantastic, always seemed to be set in an alien world: a world where running 50 or even 100 miles was considered ordinary. Yet thinking about what I've achieved over recent years, I realise that although their abilities will always be far superior to mine, I now inhabit that same domain. Especially to those on the outside looking in.

Two weeks after I ran a 53 mile race in Scotland, a casual chat with a fellow dad at my son's birthday party turned to bemusement after somebody else asked how it had gone. The screwed-up look of confusion that washed across his face was one I've become familiar with since starting to run long distances. It was a gaze of incomprehension and bewilderment, not unlike that of a child as you explain to them that daddy doesn't only drink beer because he's thirsty. "I didn't even realise people could run further than a marathon," he said. When I told him I would now run back-to-back marathons, or even further, sometimes through the night, purely for training, he just looked confused. That's when you realise your goalposts have moved.

In part, *Still Not Bionic* can be seen as a second volume to *Fat Man to Green Man* and does cover what happened next. But it also stands independent of what has gone before as it delves into the much bigger challenge of taking on 100 miles. It also explores the personal battles with my changing mental state over the span of two years and how that affected my running.

In some senses it's been a difficult book to write but it's been important and cathartic at the same time. After everything I've been through in recent years, I now appreciate that our health, both physical and mental, isn't something we should ever take for granted. What I have come to realise, more than at any other time, is that I am so far from being the invincible Six Million Dollar Man I was convinced I was as a child. At 46 years of age the sad truth I have come to accept is that I am *Still Not Bionic* and probably never will be.

Ira Rainey - *November 2016*

STILL NOT BIONIC

Prologue

It's 9:50am on a warm yet unsurprisingly wet Sunday morning in June. I'm slowly running along King's Drive in Eastbourne, which most weekends would no doubt form part of a regular route for many a local runner. However, this morning, as the heavy rain streams the sweat straight into my eyes, I appear to be on my own. As I make my way past Eastbourne District General Hospital – the grounds of which I have been explicitly instructed not to enter – I smile to myself for passing by under my own steam rather than being carried in requiring attention. I've been in many A&E departments over the years and this is one I wasn't planning on visiting.

As I approach a roundabout I look around for some small sign that I'm done, anything telling me I can finally stop running, but nothing is apparent. Spotting a familiar strip of red and white tape fluttering from a tree, I take a left at the junction followed by another immediate left onto a footpath that runs around the back of the very hospital I've just avoided. I am exhausted. Keeping my feet moving in any semblance of a running motion is an effort, yet I know I am close so I keep shuffling forwards. But as I round the corner and the only thing in sight is a long winding footpath, my resolve shatters. I slow from my lofty pace of 13 minutes per mile and resign myself to a walk.

With rain soaking my face and wipers moving across the windscreens of passing cars, it would be impossible for anyone driving past to be able to tell there were tears mixing into the raindrops on my cheeks. As I walked I simply couldn't hold back the tide of emotion that rose up within me. If anybody could see I was crying then I was beyond caring anyway. If they were uncomfortable by the sight of a soggy, balding, 46-year-old man gently weeping on the side of a main road on a Sunday morning, then that was something they would just have to deal with.

We often fight back tears but I don't know why. There is the outdated myth that to cry is to expose a weakness, particularly if you're a man. Yet there are times in my life I have cried and felt it was nothing but the right thing to do at that moment. I cried when friends have passed away; I sobbed when my children were born; and I wept uncontrollably as I gently stroked our family cat of 15 years for the last time as a vet released her from the pain of a horrible cancer. Crying in any of these instances would be considered normal, expected even, but while walking alongside the A2280 people could legitimately question what was going on.

We can never fully understand what thoughts and emotions are going through someone's head. Likewise, we have no way of knowing what journey somebody has been on or what demons they've battled by the time we cross paths with them. So making assumptions, or trying to judge the mental state of an individual, when all you have to go by is a façade is an impossible task.

As the rain drenched me that Sunday morning I wept tears of elation because I knew I was going to finish. After six months of training, more than 1,000 miles run and several pairs of trainers utterly destroyed, I absolutely knew that I was going to succeed. But it was also the end of a longer mental journey that had seen turmoil along the way. As is often the case, my joy had its foundations in darker times.

I rounded the final corner and my destination loomed into view. I wiped the rain from the screen of my watch. Time was irrelevant at this point. I was well inside the cut-off and even factoring in a degree of inaccuracy, I could see I only had half a mile left to go. The end was quite literally in sight.

Unlike the rain, my tears stopped and I smiled as I began to run for the last time - more in a final show of strength and endurance than any bid to edge down my finishing time. After all this way, nobody wants to be seen walking the last 300 metres around a running track.

Entering Eastbourne Sports Park I joined the wet track, splashing my way through the puddles, mentally ticking off each 50 metres as I went. Aware of the photographer at the finish line, I thought for a minute about how I would like to capture this moment for posterity. As I shuffled around the final bend, the chances were I was going to end up with yet another running photo where I look half dead. The reality was I looked like shit. But after not sleeping for 30 hours and having just run 100 miles over pretty much the entire length of the South Downs Way, I think I had a pretty good excuse.

STILL NOT BIONIC

1. Seeking a Century

Reflecting on the events of 2013 nobody could say it had been an ordinary year. On the positive side, I trained hard to become slimmer and fitter than I had ever been and I completed my first ultramarathon. On the negative, I lost a friend to cancer and ended up in hospital with a suspected stroke. Because misery tends to fall in threes, it probably shouldn't have been a surprise when I became physically incapacitated with a spinal problem, spending three months in a morphine-induced haze. Eventually the stroke was downgraded to a mini-stroke or, to use the correct medical term, a Transient Ischemic Attack (TIA). The issue with my back, which turned out to be a slippage of the vertebrae, lingered for a while but eventually faded away. Unfortunately it also took my hard-earned fitness with it. Although none of these problems were thought to have been directly caused by running, some questions remained unanswered. Overall it had been a very difficult year. Not just for me but also for my family. Turning the calendar to January 2014 became a metaphorical wiping clean of the slate, which would hopefully consign the issues of the previous 12 months to recent history.

As I began running again my mind automatically started to focus on finding new challenges, new adventures and distances that surpassed those I had already completed. With one ultramarathon under my belt and nobody explicitly telling me it was a bad idea to run another, I hunted around for a race that seemed like a candidate for the next logical step. I wasn't exactly sure what the next step was, but having experienced the exhilaration of crossing the finish line after running 45 miles I was hooked and knew I wanted to do it again. But this time I wanted to push myself further.

In many of the books I had read about ultras, the tales often revolved around or culminated in the magical 100-mile distance. I don't know what adding a third digit to a distance does, but it seems to elevate a race to a mystical level. One-hundred miles: that's almost four marathons back-to-back. That's crazy talk. How is it possible to cover that kind of distance on foot? How do you even begin to contemplate it? In reality it's just an arbitrary number. Being able to run 100 miles doesn't in itself change anything about the world but the very notion of it is still romantically powerful. Despite the whole idea being slightly insane, the delusional optimist in me couldn't shake the sense that it was the ultimate goal for every ultrarunner. And even with a mere single ultra finish behind me, my brain was already mapping out its route to triple digit greatness. But building up to it first was probably a good idea.

During a family trip to Scotland the previous summer, I became totally enchanted by the beauty of Trossachs National Park surrounding Loch Lomond and decided being able to run there would be amazing. The countryside was spectacular and a total departure from the trails surrounding Bristol that I was used to. After returning home I researched races in the area and found the Highland Fling. It was a race of 53 miles that followed the West Highland Way from Milngavie, just north of Glasgow, and ran right through the national park and alongside the loch itself. It looked both stunning and tough in equal measure and I was immediately sold. As soon as registrations opened I returned to the website and entered. It was exciting to have something on the calendar again.

Although I now had some experience of ultra distances, running through the Scottish Highlands was still going to be a real adventure. It might not have been the magical three-digit distance but it would hopefully be a stepping stone to bigger challenges to come. I always think adventure should be considered a relative term. But it's so often only seen as applicable for extreme challenges. Just because you're not kissing your family goodbye for a year doesn't mean that when you step outside your comfort zone that you're not being adventurous. For a child, walking to school by themselves for the first time is an adventure. Crossing roads, calling for friends, being out and about free from parental constraints… it's both exciting and nerve-racking at the same time. They're not doing anything millions of other children generations before them haven't already done, and they're certainly not pushing limits of what children are capable of, but they are testing their own boundaries and widening their experiences.

Adventure begins where your comfort zone ends; the two rarely overlap. It's about overcoming your fears and challenging yourself. While stepping free of your personal safety net can be daunting, it's where the journey begins. I realised that running ultramarathons allowed me to stand outside that zone and push my boundaries, both physically and mentally. It took me to places and offered me experiences that I just didn't get doing many other things.

Maybe in part that's because of who I am and the upbringing I had. You see, I'm an everyman, a statistical midpoint. I'm in my forties, have a family, work in an office and have a mortgage. I'm also slightly overweight and enjoy drinking beer (these two are probably related). I can't be embarrassed by any of that, it's who I am. I'm of an age and background where if anybody went away for longer than two weeks it meant prison, and the only place you could ever go to find yourself was in an A-to-Z. Trekking to the South Pole wasn't something ever discussed as a choice with my school careers advisor, not even when they knew I was studying geography at O-Level (I got a B). But I enjoyed running and liked a challenge. It was these two interests combined that offered me adventure. That was why I was going to travel 400 miles to run a further 53 miles through the green hills of Scotland.

Sean Conway, who has run, swum and cycled the length of the UK, has a nice philosophy on adventure which sums it up perfectly: "Adventure isn't all about climbing mountains or rowing oceans. Adventure, in its purest form, is simply a way of thinking!" However, if the definition of adventure is simply a mindset, what happens when a positive mental state can no longer be taken for granted?

2. Broken. Again.

The mental aspect to running ultras was something I learnt all about during my training for the Green Man Ultra. The first couple of times you ran long distances on back-to-back days you realise that despite your body telling you it wants to stop because you're tired, you need to find the strength to overrule it and keep moving forward. Sometimes that could mean just keeping your head down and relentlessly putting one foot in front of the other, and occasionally it might require stopping to have a quiet word with yourself, taking a deep breath and pushing on again. Either way, being able to deal with the constant thoughts telling you to stop is essential. But what happens when you can't control that negative thinking? More importantly: what happens when you're not in control of your mental state at all?

I can't exactly put a date to when I began to feel low. I always think 'low' sounds like a euphemism rather than something you would expect a doctor to be writing on a referral. Low mood: it just doesn't sound serious or strong enough to fully explain its power.

However, by mid-January 2014 I can definitely recall a melancholic undertone to my mood but I wasn't able to identify any significant reason why. There were certainly times when I regarded my state of mind as troubled and fleetingly considered talking to somebody, but I didn't really know who. Or about what. I did think about calling The Samaritans on more than one occasion but in the end always decided against it, feeling a lack of entitlement. Surely they were busy helping people with real issues, they didn't need me bothering them. After all, I was just a bit sad. There was absolutely an element of denial going on as well. Asking for help would mean admitting I was broken. But I wasn't, I was fine. I couldn't be depressed because I didn't have mental health issues. Had I been honest with myself, even then I would have accepted that something was already very wrong. The clouds had already gathered and it was getting darker.

At the start of March 2014, six weeks before the Highland Fling - even with the training I had been doing - there wasn't much improvement in my state of mind. Despite running supposedly delivering benefits for mental health, I was harbouring a dulling sadness. Something I continued to keep to myself. Like a fool I thought that if I just ignored the sorrow it would go away. Only it didn't.

I don't recollect the start of Thursday, 13 March 2014 as being a day of any particular note. It began like any other Thursday. I got up, readied myself for work and set off on my regular commute to Bath. I certainly don't recall leaving home in such an obvious state of mind as to be able to predict what was to happen during that routine drive. What I do remember, with vivid clarity, is driving down a country road and fixating on the truck approaching me on the opposite side. And then steering my car across the white line into its path.

Looking back with a clear head I can only say it was a deliberate act. But the definition of doing something deliberately implies you've considered the consequences of the action you are about to undertake. That doesn't describe what happened before I turned the steering wheel. Yet turn it I did. Or at least some part of me did. Committing suicide that morning wasn't something that had been on my conscious agenda but unfortunately the reasoned part of my brain didn't have absolute control.

Almost as quickly as I turned out of my lane, I swerved back across to the left-hand side and pulled straight into a lay-by. I sat shaking at what had just happened. What *had* happened? In the moment of realisation and adrenaline that followed, it became clear the veneer of denial I was using to hide my broken state of mind needed to be torn down. I had to accept the fact I needed help. Admitting that to myself, I sat in the car on the side of the road and cried. I didn't go in to work that day. In fact I didn't go to work for the best part of the next month.

My diagnosis, after the initial consultation with the mental health service I was referred to, was that of severe depression. In a twisted way it was a relief. I could give up the lie I had been telling myself. There was now a definition to my sadness. This meant I was legitimately able to ask for help.

In the weeks that followed I barely left the house. Some days I got up along with everybody else in the pretence of a normal existence. But once my family had all left for the day, I would return to the safety of the duvet and stay tucked in until just before they came home again. On the days I did stay up, I simply lay on the floor for hours with my cat cuddled up beside me. The floor felt like a safe place to be.

The sharp peak of depression had numbed my enthusiasm and enjoyment of everything. An indescribable sense of hopelessness made feeling anything impossible. I became numb to life. It's so easy to look back when you're in a positive state of mind and see through the gloom, to want to be able to tell your earlier self that it would be alright, but at the time you can't see anything. There is only an all-pervading darkness of disenchantment with life.

I was prescribed anti-depressant medication, and after taking them for a number of weeks they began to take effect and eventually began to help. My doctor told me the drugs weren't any kind of a cure but were more like receiving a warm ray of sunshine on your brain. They were something to help you feel you have a reason to smile. As I began to accept the illness and its presence, I tried to get back to as normal a routine as possible. Even then I didn't have a full and open discussion with everyone. For lots of people who know me, reading this will be the first they will have heard of any illness. No doubt that will raise concerns among a few, but the main reason I didn't tell many others was mostly because there never seemed a good time to bring it up. It's an awkward conversation to start. "Alright? Oh, by the way did I tell you I tried to kill myself by driving in front of a truck the other day? How're the kids?"

Depression and other mental health issues are still rarely discussed among the wider population. In part this is down to a lack of comprehension, and in part embarrassment and discomfort when talking about them. It's a subject that remains stigmatised and misunderstood. But it's important to realise these are illnesses and not character traits. We should be able to talk about mental health in the same way we would any physical ailment, yet we can't. This is partly why I wanted to write this book. I wanted to honestly share my thoughts, feelings and experiences. If reading about what I have been through helps even one person face up to their own denial, then it's absolutely been worth writing this.

After a few long weeks of hiding away I tentatively eased my way back to running and the outside world. I had begun a course of Cognitive Behaviour Therapy (CBT), which alongside the medication and getting back outdoors and being active was enough to help me attempt a return to normality and to go back to work. CBT is a talking therapy based on the belief that problems aren't caused by events but how you interpret them in your head. It's these thoughts that affect us in a negative way. The therapy was a huge help. Where I would have once sneered at words like 'toolkit' to help with my mental state, I now consider the skills I learnt from the CBT sessions invaluable. The idea you can possess a set of tools to help you fix your thoughts is an excellent analogy. While CBT doesn't help everybody, it taught me how to change the way I view things and to identify and challenge my negative thinking. More importantly, it helped me face up to my illness.

Recognising and being able to deal with negative thought patterns isn't just a technique for helping to deal with depression and anxiety, but also something that crosses all areas of life. Running long distances takes a lot of mental endurance and you find yourself dealing with the demons in your head while you run. With the Highland Fling only a few weeks away, I couldn't shy away from the fact that my training had been affected by everything that had happened and that I hadn't run as many miles in training as I would've liked. But with the promise of the adventure that the race would deliver, I thought it was important to go and tackle it anyway. Even if my physical fitness wasn't where it should be, I couldn't help but wonder if my new mental toolkit could help me through the Highlands of Scotland.

STILL NOT BIONIC

3. Steak, Tablet, Steak

I've always found it comical how even on short flights an airline will still try to sell you overpriced snacks and drinks. Our flying time from Bristol to Glasgow was just one hour and 15 minutes, yet out came the drinks trolley anyway. Between climbing and descent the stewardess barely had time to dash down the aisle offering up her nuts for sale. Luckily I'd already polished off a compulsory cooked airport breakfast, even though my flight was mid-afternoon.

Joining me on the trip to Scotland were my former Green Man running partner Bear Schlenker, and ultra newbie Paul Wootten. While the Highland Fling was Paul's first foray into the world of ultramarathons, it wasn't his first long run having already run several marathons, including one along the particularly unrunnable Great Wall of China. In spite of only running together for a short time, we had been friends for more than 30 years, having been in the same class at school. We now lived within two miles of each other, and by a fateful twist of birthdays our daughters were also classmates. Despite his unfathomable love for Bristol Rovers football club and Vespa scooters, we got on well and had the same laidback approach to life. The only problem was, with all his reckless ideas and madcap plans, my wife considered him to be a bad influence. Then again, his wife felt the same about me. It seemed like a good balance.

While the long winter months of training hadn't gone quite as smoothly as I had originally planned, and I wasn't as fit as I was the year before, I had done some running. Whether it was enough to tackle 53 miles of the West Highland Way we would have to wait and see.

After arriving in Glasgow, we took a short taxi ride and found ourselves in Milngavie: the elusive town that had been sitting on the horizon of reality for so long. It seemed like a lifetime ago that I had entered the race because so much had happened since then. Returning to work and not isolating myself from everything was helping me gain a semblance of normality. I found the medication was helping and it gave me the drive to get on with life again.

After checking into our hotel we walked into town and strolled around the small centre, quickly finding the start of the path subtly located under a huge sign. Looking for a calorie-filled lunch we went into Greggs the bakers and bought a selection of their finest delicacies. Rather than using the internationally recognised method of payment, i.e. cash, Paul caused havoc with his new-fangled Greggs iPhone app. After much confusion, till beating, swearing and the formation of a sizable angry queue of Scots, he walked out with a free pasty.

As a small town we found all the sights pretty quickly: the obelisk, the underpass where the race starts, and the car park next to the train station where we had to drop off our bags in the morning. It was all pretty familiar after spending months watching YouTube videos, reading blog posts and studying all the race photos I could find. We popped into Tesco to load up with supplies for the next day. Up and down the aisles we strolled looking for all manner of sugary and savoury treats that would fuel us around the 53 miles of Highland countryside. I stocked up with Coke, jaffa cakes, pork pies and, taking inspiration from being in Scotland, I picked up several packets of tablet.

If you haven't heard of tablet before, think of it as stale fudge on crack. Legend has it they were originally making fudge but the mix went badly wrong so they just added more sugar. The result is a bit like Kendal Mint Cake without the mint. And more sugar. It's an ideal item to have in your bag for running due to its high sugary content. The only trouble is if you eat more than four bars in any single day you run the risk of falling into a diabetic coma, turning your blood into golden syrup and seeing through time. On Saturday, I ate five.

Back at the hotel we packed up our drop bags with both sugary and salty treats and rested for the afternoon. As evening rolled around, we headed to the pub down the road to collect our race numbers and timing chips. It was a very informal event and we took the opportunity to feast on steak and chips. As other runners sat around with bowls of pasta, or healthy looking dinners, we tucked into a plate of meat and potatoes, washed down with a beer. It was something that had become a standard pre-race meal for Paul and me. Not that there was any particular physiological benefit to eating steak the night before a long run, we just really like steak. After all, a night away is a night away, whether you're racing the next day or not.

With everything packed and ready for the morning we opted for an early night of not much sleep. As the alarm went off at 4am, I jumped out of bed convinced I had a million things to do. I didn't of course, as I had prepared everything the night before. It was simply nervous energy kicking in early. While being anxious about running 53 miles is an entirely natural feeling, there was nothing more I could do now. I sat on the end of my bed watching a kettle slowly boil, waiting for my bowels to wake up and trying to convince myself I liked porridge. Pre-race nutrition is an important part of setting up your day before a long run, and although I wasn't convinced by the watery, clumping oats, being in Scotland I gave it a go. I was right the first time. With it still being too early to go down to the restaurant for a full cooked option, I topped up with some jaffa cakes instead.

All week, in the run up to the event, I'd had been keeping a close eye on the weather forecast and it had been promising to be entirely wet for Saturday. With heavy rain in places. This wasn't unsurprising for Scotland in April. The trouble with looking at forecasts for ultra events is that, because of the distances being covered, you need to check the weather over several locations. Even with that considered, we readied ourselves for a soaking.

As we left the hotel for the short stroll to the start, there was happily no sign of rain. Ambling down to the train station, we handed over our drop bags stuffed with extra food and supplies at the relevant vans, ready to be carted off around the Highlands for collection later. There was an incredible amount of people milling about, proving just how popular this race was. There were around 650 starters, making it sizable for any kind of running event let alone an ultramarathon. While the popularity of ultrarunning had been on the rise for a number of years, it was still uncommon to see more than 200-300 runners on a start line. With this still being only my second ultra event, it was something of a surprise. My only experience of such events so far was the Green Man, which had been so much smaller with a select field of just 65 runners. But the large pack of runners didn't change our plan. The three of us agreed before the event that this wasn't about the time. Sure we wanted to run as best we could, but we also wanted to enjoy it.

Just before 6am we huddled together in the underpass ready for the start. There were hundreds of people out lining the route, cheering us on. You wouldn't have been able to get into Greggs if you wanted to. As we began to run, we passed through the centre of town, past the closed shops, before turning off onto the start of the West Highland Way. Leaving the shops behind, the path instantly turned into trail running beside a river and disappeared into woodland. Our journey had begun.

Unlike when training for the Green Man, I hadn't been able to recce any of the route. It was all something of an unknown. But everyone had told me the path was well marked and the event fully marshalled, so I went into it with an element of blind faith. This was a conscious decision following on from the disruption of spending much of March lying on the floor with my cat. I decided not to put any undue pressure on myself and decided not to make a race plan or even wear a watch. I wouldn't know how long I'd been running, nor would I know how far I'd gone. I figured if I hadn't reached the finish, then I needed to keep moving until I got there. I was running simply for fun and scenery.

Other than turning right into a field at four miles and seeing some distant hills shrouded in low cloud, the first ten miles were pretty uneventful. We plodded along thinking how it was all nicely pleasant but not exceptional. I hoped it would improve with distance. With running ultras still being something new for the three of us, lots of folk were keen to follow our progress so I decided to try and keep people informed by updating Twitter along the way. The idea started out with a few snaps and messages as we began moving, and it was great to read the replies of good luck roll back in. However, the sporadic nature of the phone signal once we moved away from civilisation meant the updates were less frequent than planned.

Then the race changed. At around 16 miles we came up to the legendary Conic Hill. I had read about it and people had warned me of it, but nothing prepared me for getting up close and personal on it. From the bottom we could just make out a train of dots edging their way up the side. Tiny people were disappearing into the cloud masking the summit. At that point there hadn't been any serious climbs. This was the first, but at more than 1,000 feet it certainly made up for the earlier deficit. As we slowly walked our way to the top, there was a real sense we were going to be rewarded with a view. Spying a photographer perched near the top we broke into a few steps of a mock run in the pretence of running to the brow of the hill. We laughed at our incredible wit and he smiled the smile of a man who'd seen the same thing 300 times already that day.

As if timed to perfection, the clouds had begun to clear and the sun was attempting to break through. It coincided perfectly with us reaching the pinnacle of the hill. Wow! This was what I came here for. This was the scenery that had so enticed me the year before. The view from the top was simply spectacular with the majesty of Loch Lomond laid out before us, flanked by thick green woodland. Instantly the whole race changed. From running along low trails and through woods, we were now high up in the hills at the start of the loch, with a steep descent down to the first checkpoint ahead of us. Still grinning, we carefully bounced our way down to our first drop bag at the water's edge.

At Balmaha we picked up our bags and sat for a few minutes beside the loch on a picnic bench, tucking into our treats from the day before. Munching on a mixture of pork pies and tablet, I found it funny watching the other runners. One after the other they ran in, grabbed their bag and ran out again. It was like watching a train of white rabbits from *Alice in Wonderland*, all late for a very important date. Part of me wondered if we were missing something.

Snacks packed back away we moved on. We plodded our way along shingle beaches and muddy paths just feet from the water's edge. It was a stunning location to be running in and it was impossible not to smile as we passed through the halfway point.

Our second bag drop was located at Rowardennan, around the 28 mile mark. With the awe of the scenery having softened slightly, this was when I began to suffer. At the checkpoint I sat on the wall at the edge of the loch and tried to eat something but I had started to feel sick. My stomach was hurting and I felt more than a bit queasy. Maybe I'd eaten too much tablet? Leaving the marshals behind as we set off, my head ventured into negative places and the idea of dropping out flashed through my mind. I struggled to keep up with Paul and Bear over the next section and became increasingly concerned with what was still to come. My confidence had started to fade and I let them pull away. This gave me an excuse to slow my pace

3. STEAK, TABLET, STEAK

and battle my inner monologue. We still had more than 20 miles to go and feeling this shit now was far from ideal. The euphoria of the top of Conic Hill was long gone and I was struggling to keep going. Both physically and mentally.

The next section along the edge of the loch was rocky and technical, making consistent running hard work. This suited me and I was happy to start to lose sight of the people in front, keeping to myself. The next checkpoint was located at the Inversnaid Hotel, which was at 34 miles. Not wearing a watch or GPS I had no real idea where I was or how long I had been running for. I didn't even know when to expect the next checkpoint to arrive. So when I asked a runner coming up behind me how far it was to Inversnaid, I was delighted to hear: "About 400 metres".

Rounding the corner, the large white hotel sitting on the side of the loch was a beautiful sight to behold. Bear and Paul were waiting for me. I sat on the ground and had a rest. With the slower pace I had started to feel a little better and managed to eat a bit more. I asked somebody to take a picture of the three of us, which turned out to be the death of my phone battery. No problem I thought, I had an external battery and promptly dug it out of my bag. The trouble was I had forgotten to pack the cable. That was the end of the photos and the updates.

Leaving Inversnaid, the terrain became even more technical and much of the route between there and the final checkpoint at Beinglas Farm, at around 40 miles, involved climbing over large rocks and through waterfalls. It was incredibly scenic but exceptionally slow going. Having battled back my negative thinking, I found a second wind and felt rejuvenated. While Paul, Bear and I didn't care too much about our finishing time, we did have a loose expectation of about 12 hours in mind. Though it was clear by now that that wasn't going to happen. The terrain was much hillier and more technical than we had envisaged and progress was slow. What had also become apparent throughout the course of the day was that our checkpoint approach of sitting down and having a picnic was in stark contrast to that of everyone else. We probably lost at least 30 minutes from our snack stops alone. Definitely something to learn from.

By the time we reached the checkpoint at Beinglas Farm, there weren't a huge amount of other runners still around us. We stopped for a while, finding a Ginsters Peppered Steak slice among the leftovers of previous runners, something that happily refuelled Paul. Leaving the marshals behind, and with 40 miles in the bank, we only had a half marathon left to go. Unfortunately it wasn't a flat one. After running through the aptly named Cow Poo Alley, we followed a fairly nondescript and undulating section of the route slight north of the A82 before coming to our final hill challenge of the day, affectionately known as the rollercoaster. To say that this section was well named is something of an understatement. By this stage, Bear had pulled away while Paul and I had been reduced to a gentle stroll up the hills and through the woodland. Coming down the final descent, we passed under a railway bridge and crossed the road onto flatter terrain. Level ground: it was a welcome sight. By now we had reached the 50 mile mark and the end was tantalisingly close.

Ambling along, talking with a group of others, we were all ready for it to now be over. We strolled for a bit before picking it up and slowly stumbling our way through the final section of forest. Jogging past the lone piper (a nice touch), we rounded the final corner to see a finish line. After 53 miles of trail hills, woodland and rocks, we were now presented by a red carpet lined by a cheering crowd and framed by a welcoming inflatable arch. It was truly surreal and a thing of beauty. We picked up our pace to a plod, knowing we could almost stop, high-fiving people as we ran our way across the finish line. We had done it. Fifty-three miles in the bank in a time of 13 hours and 31 minutes. Bear finished strongly 20 minutes ahead of us.

As we crossed under the arch, we had our timing chips removed and strolled casually into the tent to collect our bag of swag. For the money the event cost to enter, the goody bag was amazing. It was one of the best from any event I'd run in nearly 15 years. There was the obligatory medal, technical t-shirt, a Buff, bottle of bubbly and even a Highland Fling sticker (affixed to the laptop I'm writing this on). But that wasn't all. Shuffle along to the next table and there was free beer, hot soup and bread rolls. There was also a complimentary massage if you wanted it. It was like an oasis of fun after 53 miles of joyful punishment. To top all that off there was a coach waiting to take us back to Milngavie. It's only when the bus journey back to the start takes an hour and a half that you realise just how far you've run.

By the time we got back to our hotel and I had plugged my phone back in, I had several missed calls, 14 text messages and a huge number of Tweets - mostly wondering what had happened and asking if were we still alive. Yes, we were. As I sat there tucking into another large T-bone steak and chips, washed down with plenty of beer, I replied to all those messages informing them all we had done it. We weren't the fastest and we weren't the slowest, but we had completed all 53 miles and had absolutely loved it.

Reflecting on the weekend, looking back at photos after I got home, my wife commented on how it was the happiest I had looked for many months. While there had definitely been several low points along the way, overall the experience had been exactly what I needed. Running with Bear and Paul we had laughed, joked and put the world to rights over the course of the day. Even better were the total strangers who volunteered their precious time by standing in car parks and on farms providing logistical and moral support for runners they had never met. It was an incredible community of supportive folk who helped make the day so great.

Being physically active, spending time connecting with friends and being mindful of the present moment and your surroundings were all things that I had read were important in aiding your mental wellbeing. This event had certainly provided all of that. Interestingly, giving to others, through small acts of kindness or time spent volunteering can also improve your mood. The marshals out on the course certainly fitted into that category and their time and support also had a knock-on for the mood of the runners. It was something to remember for sure. Overall the whole event had been life affirming and exactly what I needed.

4. Blood, Blood, Glorious Blood

A few weeks after returning from romping around the Scottish Highlands, I sat with my doctor to discuss how I had been feeling. After the highs of the race I noticed my mood slowly start to decline again. Despite everything, I began to feel low again and recognised the familiar senses of lethargy, disinterest and despondency creeping back in. I was relapsing. But this time I identified it and didn't delay in talking to somebody. As well as the CBT and anti-depressants, regular reviews were part of the ongoing treatment. I had a good relationship with my GP and found talking to him easy. He listened, was helpful and tolerated my incessant questioning. The decision was taken to double my dose of medication and see if that helped. There were other drugs to try if need be but it was also important to realise they didn't work for everyone. Only time would tell if I was one of them.

The previous year I had spent a lot of time in my doctor's surgery after suffering a TIA, blood clots in my lungs and a debilitating back problem. While the issues had all eventually cleared up, my GP still wasn't happy with not knowing what caused them, particularly the TIA and the clots. With more races already being pencilled in, he decided trying to discover if I had an underlying condition that put me at risk, or could cause a recurrence, was probably a good idea. That meant taking a closer look at my blood.

Several weeks later, sitting at Southmead Hospital in Bristol waiting for my appointment with a blood specialist, I couldn't help but be reminded of the week I spent on the stroke ward in Bath. Until the previous year, I hadn't spent any significant amount of time in hospital, yet since then I had become a frequent visitor. Could that be a by-product of getting older, or was ultrarunning just not good for me? Every now and then, somebody would helpfully inform me running was actually bad for you, especially as I got older. But I remained optimistic. Running and keeping active was playing an important part in helping me manage my depression and I wasn't planning on stopping any time soon.

As I had previously been diagnosed with blood clots, the starting point was to determine how they could have developed. Could I have a genetic clotting disorder? Was that how a small part of a clot could have made it to my brain, causing the TIA? It was unlikely, but it was still worth investigating and hopefully ruling out.

The first step was to run some tests that would identify any abnormal clotting factors. The second was to import the chest scans from the hospital in Bath and re-examine them more closely. After going over my medical and family history, combined with my discharge notes from the stroke unit, the haematology consultant was already sceptical of the original diagnosis.

Two months later, with the tests results back, I returned to Southmead for a review of the findings. Having imported the original chest scans, they had been reviewed by somebody whose opinion was trusted implicitly by the haematologist. The resulting conversation was something of a surprise, and probably would've been funny if I hadn't spent six months on anti-coagulant drugs and going without beer the previous summer. The outcome was that no conclusive proof of blood clots could be found on the scans. Combined with the initial lack of symptoms, it seemed the original diagnosis was in doubt. The exact words used were slightly more colourful than the official letter written back to my GP but the outcome was the same. As far as several consultants were now concerned, no clear evidence existed. In simple terms, I had never had any clots in my lungs. It was something of a shock but a pleasant one nonetheless. It turns out I was a little less broken than I thought. However, it didn't get us any closer to what had caused the TIA.

We talked about running and the risk of blood clots and the haematologist told me about risk factors for athletes. These included blood thickening through dehydration, inflammation of the blood vessels, and the dangers of long distance travel, or low heart rate and low blood pressure. In layman's terms, the combination of becoming dehydrated, damaging veins and arteries through prolonged activity, and having a lower heart rate because you are fit, all increase your risk of developing clots. It's something athletes of all levels should be aware of. If you want to find out more, do an internet search for 'Virchow's triad for athletes'.

Reducing the chance of developing clots is fairly straightforward. When running, be conscious of your thirst. Make sure you drink plenty of water and electrolytes both during and after. Try to break up long journeys, and remember to move about and stretch on flights or other prolonged travel. It's fairly common advice but could be life-saving. Dehydration is something that can creep up on you when out running, particularly during the warmer months. This is why it's always good to take long runs seriously. Something I was guilty of not always doing.

STILL NOT BIONIC

5. Falling Down on Solsbury Hill

As we moved through July, with the Highland Fling already a distant memory, I found myself a little light on mileage. It hadn't been a conscious decision, more just feeling apathetic about running. With the increase in dosage of anti-depressants my mood had improved over the previous months and on the whole I was feeling positive about most things. Running just didn't seem to be one of them. Normally that wouldn't be a problem as it's good to have some downtime after a race, but it was more than two months since returning from Scotland and I had the small matter of another 45 mile ultra to run in just over four weeks. I needed to get some miles in. So when Paul said he had a spare place for the Bath Running Festival Marathon in July I thought 'why not?' It was only a week until the trail race but I figured it would be fine. Wouldn't it?

Having not run more than 12 miles since April, I knew I would be running on mental strength alone. I was comfortable with that though. It would be another test of mental endurance. After experiencing a full range of emotions in Scotland, I drew on what I'd learnt in dealing with negative thinking to help get me through when my body was telling me to quit. I was planning on treating this race just like a short ultra – slow, steady and with lots of cake.

What I hadn't factored for, however, was quite how hilly the course was. I'm not talking a touch of undulation here, but real, serious hills. Climbs with a view. The day before the race I was talking to a friend who would normally finish a marathon in three hours and even *he* was only hoping for a four-and-a-half hour finish. It sounded tough. Tougher than I had expected when I accepted the place.

Bath is a hilly city. That much is an indisputable fact. It's nestled in a valley probably carved eons ago by some Ice Age glacier or something equally geological that I didn't understand. This is why the biggest half marathon in the city runs around some of its blandest parts: to keep it flat, fast and popular. But if you embrace the hills you can truly enjoy the city's majesty, which is exactly what the summer running festival organised by Relish Running does. The festival is a series of trail runs covering various distances from children's races right up to the marathon I was running. All races started and finished at the high point of the University of Bath campus and, depending on the distance covered, a whole range of terrain was just waiting to be tackled. Hills, however, were not optional.

Setting off early, Paul and I drove to Bath, arriving at the university ready to ditch the car and collect our race numbers. That sorted we sat about on the grass taking in the sun for a while, waiting for the races to begin. First the half marathon runners went off, and there were a lot of them. It was called a half marathon but it was actually about 16 miles in length. It was definitely more challenging than the popular road half marathon most runners in Bath might have experienced. Shortly after, a brave collection of around 200 runners lined up for the marathon. It was turning into a hot day so staying hydrated was going to be particularly important. Words of warning from the haematologist were already ringing in the back of my head, so I made a mental note to ensure my bottles were always refilled at each checkpoint even if they weren't empty.

To the sound of an air horn we ran off into the woods like picnicking bears rushing for the best spot. At this point it struck me I had absolutely no idea where the course went. I was going to have to follow people in front and hope the route was well marked out. Looping around the university grounds and down into the woods, the pack I was in all stopped, thinking we had gone the wrong way. It wasn't just Paul and me, but a group of about 40 runners. We knew we were lost for sure when we saw another group coming back up the other way, telling us that was definitely the wrong direction. Clearly a common navigational blunder by all.

Making our way out of the woods towards a stile is where I first rolled my ankle. I yelped quietly as I went over on it and the pain shot up my leg. I stood there for a couple of minutes as people streamed past me asking if I was all right. I wasn't but in a typically British way I naturally said I was. As the throbbing eased, I hobbled over the stile and walked a little before picking it up into a jog. When the pain had faded a touch, I realised I needed to be more careful going forward or I could end up in real trouble. I caught up with Paul and we ran down the hill and along the canal in the direction of Batheaston. This was where we began our first climb up Fosse Lane. What started out as a short steep road turned into a never-ending uphill grind. Turning from tarmac to gravel and then to dirt, it just kept going up.

From the top we ran through a few fields, down a steep wooded lane before reaching the joy of our second hill. Words fail me when I think about this climb. It wasn't really a hill at all, more a wall with roots sticking out of it. It was like part of the world had fallen away into oblivion and we had to run up what was left. There was no clearly defined trail or tarmac road to run up, it was simply a steep mud and rock gully that climbed to infinity and beyond. I took one look up and decided it was definitely a walker. I say walk but what I really mean is crawl on all fours. For ages. This hill could best be described as bullshit. Looking at the GPS data afterwards it seems the climb was only about half a mile long… but with a 24 percent incline. That's a climb that would burn out a stairlift.

We scaled our way up the gully to the roof of the Earth, thankful it was at least shaded from the hot sun. Reaching the top we were greeted by the beautiful sight of a checkpoint. I can only imagine it had been dropped in by helicopter. I had no idea where we were but it felt like Tibet, only with jaffa cakes. "That's the last proper hill you've got," the marshal said. That was of course a lie but at the time it was a very welcome one.

It wasn't long after leaving the checkpoint, running over uneven ground that I went over on my ankle for the second time. With it already being tender, I went down like a sack of screaming spuds. Rolling about on the floor in agony, it felt as if my foot had been torn from my leg. Several people stopped to see if I was all right but by the time they reached me I was already up and hopping towards a nearby stile. At that point, only 11 miles in, I thought my race was over. Stopping on a fence, I took a couple of painkillers and rested for a few minutes before hobbling off in the direction of the race. I wasn't going to quit. Besides, I was miles from anywhere and needed to get back to civilisation somehow, so I just carried on.

Gingerly I edged downhill through some woodland, before having to trek up yet another hill. It was definitely a hill. I had absolutely been lied to at the last checkpoint. This time we were on top of Solsbury Hill (of Peter Gabriel fame). Looking out over Bath below, I couldn't recognise a single landmark. It was all so small and so far away. Paul and I paused to take in the view and pose for a couple of photos. Running on, we ran down a Tarmac lane so steep it was painful on the knees and quads alike. But at the bottom we found ourselves back on familiar ground, at the checkpoint in Batheaston. It was a welcome sight. We stopped, knocked back some flat Coke, filled our bottles and munched more flapjacks before ploughing on.

By now my ankle wasn't feeling too bad. It was swollen and sore but running on it didn't cause me any trouble. I just didn't want to make it three times unlucky and roll it again. With the marathon and half marathon following the same route, we had now started to catch people running the half: brave souls who had battled the heat and the hills up and were basking in the glory of being only a few miles away from being able to stop. We marathoners, however, had no such luxury. Where the marathon differed from the half was that at the 14.5 mile point we had to turn around and take on all those glorious hills for a second time.

The turning point had a cut-off of three-and-a-half hours, which we were told would be strictly enforced. At the start of the race we scoffed at such a liberal time, but now coming along the canal path with half a mile still to go and the clock showing three hours and ten minutes, the smile had been wiped from our faces. We collected our bands proving we had reached the turning point, scoffed on some more goodies and set back off along the dusty towpath to return to our hilly fate.

As with any journey, the second time around the course somehow seemed shorter. When I say that, I mean the hills just came upon us quicker. Once again we walked and crawled our way up the climbs. This time around I began talking to a runner who lived in Borneo and was over in the UK running the event with his daughter. Talking about trail running I asked him if he needed to be careful of the wildlife when running in the forests of Borneo, which he confirmed was the case. "So is it the snakes you need to be careful of?" I asked. "No, the snakes are OK," he said. "It's the elephants you need to watch out for." Noted.

Slowly we made our way back around the course. We had made the cut-off so now it was just a case of making it to the end. At this point, providing I didn't go over on my ankle again, I knew the finish was coming. It wouldn't be pretty and it certainly wouldn't be fast, but finish I would. Coming back down through Bathampton for the last time, we ran back past a crammed pub nestled on the side of the canal. It was the same pub we had run past four times in the space of one race. The beer garden, still full of people bewildered by what we were doing, cheered as we passed by once more. A couple of miles later, we turned off the canal with only a mile to go. Despite that final mile being entirely uphill, there was nothing they could throw at us now that would be worse than what we had already done. Our spirits hadn't been broken yet and they weren't going to be now. We climbed back into the university grounds and followed the looping paths around to the finish. Emerging through a huddle of trees, I spied the low-key finishing funnel, pushed my shoulders back and ran strong across the line.

The winner of the race, local GB marathon and ultra runner Holly Rush, crossed the finish line in a touch over three-and-a-half hours. We followed shortly behind her… two-and-a-half hours later. It was easily the slowest marathon I'd ever run, but with around 3,600 feet of ascent (and the same descent) it was absolutely the hilliest, too. With the absence of any training, it was never going to be about the time, instead it was about confidence. I took it steady and even felt like I could have done more at the end. Had it been an ultra and I had to go back out for a third lap then I'm sure I could. It wouldn't have been pretty but I could have done it.

It is of course undeniable that if you want to go out and run fast times in road races, it would be beneficial to train plenty and take it seriously. But if you want to get out on the trails and challenge yourself, and not just focus on the clock, then you can be a little more liberal. Once again I had proved to myself that with a positive mindset I could push on when the going was tough (even with a twisted ankle). There was a time when I wouldn't have dreamt of running a marathon without three or four months of solid training, and even then it would floor me for weeks afterwards. How different this had been. Next up would be 45 miles in the dark.

6. The Fields Have Eyes

As a child, I avoided the dark at all costs. With my bedroom door ajar and my shadowy monster-shaped dressing gown taken down from its hook, the light from the bathroom bulb shone just enough salvation into my room to hold the darkness at bay. Each night, as my parents climbed the stairs to bed, they thoughtlessly switched off the light that had been left on. However, the moment their bedroom door closed I would leap out of bed like a nyctophobic ninja and yank the plastic-toggled string switching it straight back on again. Maybe I just watched too much *Scooby Doo* but I was never a fan of the night. Being honest, even at 46 I still harboured a slightly irrational fear of the dark. How could you not be even a little scared of what you can't see? It just wasn't right. Certainly the idea of going out running through the woods between the hours of dusk and dawn didn't hold any appeal whatsoever. At least, I didn't think it did.

When I first heard about the Green Man Midnight Express, I was surprised by how attracted I was to running it. The event followed the same wooded 45 mile loop of Bristol as the Green Man Ultra, albeit in the opposite direction, and starting - as the name implied - at midnight. Despite most of my brain telling me I really should stay indoors with the lights on, there was still a tiny masochistic niggle pushing me to face up to my phobia. Running an ultra through the hours of darkness - the darksome night, full of shadow, murk and gloom - was a double barrel of mental endurance. But like a moth to a bulb, it was an idea I felt strangely drawn to.

Being well acquainted with the route, it seemed like an ideal opportunity to gain some night running experience in a familiar environment. The bigger truth was, with the idea of entering a 100 mile race persistently floating around in my head, I knew that night running would eventually be unavoidable. Knowing whether I could actually tolerate it would be useful before writing cheques my head couldn't cash.

Whether lots of ultra runners are scared of the dark, or because it was the first year for the event, the numbers at the start were only small. Just ten plucky souls stood in the small village hall at Norton Malreward that August bank holiday weekend. Ten people who, for one reason or another, decided running 45 miles through the night was their best option for a Friday night. Bonkers or not, there was an atmosphere and friendly camaraderie that only a band of runners heading out to circumnavigate a sleeping city could generate.

Looking around the room I realised I already knew most of the people there. While the popularity of ultrarunning globally is on the increase, on a local level it is surprising how often you cross paths with the same people. A few were old friends and some I had met at the Green Man Ultra the year before. Importantly, everyone already knew the route, having run it at least once before.

I had also persuaded Guy Lucas, who ran the Green Man followed by the Bath Half Marathon the previous year with Bear and me to run. He drove over to my house after work, and following a hearty pasta dinner we were just as ready for a sleep as much as a long run. Being tired from running was one thing, but staying awake after you've already been up and at work all day was another.

Running through the night is a very different experience to taking on an early morning race. Not only do you have to contend with navigation in the dark but also the increasing tiredness and desire to curl up in a ditch and have a snooze. Having never worked shifts, nor been much of a party animal, I can only remember one occasion when I had previously stayed up all night. But watching *Yo!*

MTV Raps until the sun came up as a rebellious 20-year-old because my parents were on holiday was a world away from this.

Following a whispered countdown outside some very expensive looking cottages, the race began and we snaked through a kissing gate into the first dark field. The short train of head torches moving along the path quickly stretched out. It was clear from the outset that this was going to be a race of two halves. A leading pack would blaze a trail through the forest at a blistering pace, and a group of also-rans would bring up the rear. I was happily in the latter. In our perfectly formed little gang along with Guy and myself was also Claire (the wife of my original ultrarunning sage Bill Graham) and Jim Smith. I hadn't met Jim before but I had spoken to him online a number of times. After *Fat Man to Green Man* was published, Jim had got in touch saying he had also run the same double-header weekend as we did the previous year. It seemed I wasn't the only one to follow through on crazy ideas.

As a delusional optimist, one of my core traits is to not overly think things through. This isn't down to any lack of planning or attention to detail, merely an overarching sense that actually, it will just be all right. Whatever it is, I'll work it out. I think it's a simple defence mechanism to stop my brain from becoming burdened with so much noise it can't decide on anything. It's not dissimilar to something I learnt from CBT. Which is that if something is worrying you and you perceive it to be a problem, ask yourself if you can do anything about it? If you can, then do, but if you can't, then let it go. If it's outside of your control, worrying about it is futile and achieves nothing.

The heavy breathing and muted sounds that emanated from the shadows as we began to cross the next field were both worrying and something we could take action on. Run. As the noise got closer, it was joined by the dull thundering of a thousand bovine hooves. Our group gathered in tight and ran faster as a pack. Turning my head to the left as I ran, the beam from my head torch was reflected back from countless pairs of glistening green eyes. Hovering eyes that were gaining ground on us. Who, or what, owned the eyes wasn't something we were going to stick around to find out. I don't know which raced more through that field, my legs or my heart.

The first important lesson I learnt from my inaugural night running adventure was that fields which look empty probably aren't. You never know what is hiding in the blackness waiting to chase you. There is nothing creepier than seeing a herd of glowing eyes coming towards you out of the dark. Scream if you like but that might just spook them all the more. So just keep moving.

Leaving the farms of Dundry behind, we made our way down the hill, across the A38 and through into Ashton Court Estate. Running up past the mansion house we entered the deer enclosure, up to the Green Man head itself and on over Brunel's famous suspension bridge. At this point we were about 12 miles in and we had long ago lost sight of the faster runners leading the charge. In a strange way I always find that quite comforting. Rather than feeling as if I'm floundering hopelessly at the back, I don't feel the pressure to keep up with those in front. Trying to maintain an uncomfortable and unsustainable pace can kill a race very quickly. By the time we reached the next largely rural part of the path, around Easter Compton at about 20 miles, I found myself not even thinking about the darkness. With hours still to pass before the sun would come up I was happily jogging through woodland, graveyards and fields alike without a care in the world. Maybe it was just the distraction of keeping running, but through some form of exposure therapy the darkness wasn't bothering me at all.

Around the halfway point our group split again, leaving just Jim and myself bringing up the rear. I was perfectly happy with that, and despite Jim having run the event in the daytime he was still looking to better his previous time. As we ran we talked shit, taking in everything from race experiences, tattoos, our love of beer and trying to keep a happy family balance. It was all familiar and common ground and we were coming from the same place. The conversation helped the miles drift by and made the small fact we were traversing the night incidental. While running for many hours at a time is never an easy pursuit, it is definitely made easier when you're in good company.

Leaving the third checkpoint at Hambrook at around 5:30am we headed for Keynsham and the final checkpoint. The sun had started to rise, which after running almost 30 miles in the dark was a moment we had been waiting for. Everything I'd read suggested that sunrise was a magical time that would re-energise you. But I beg to differ. Seeing the sun come back up after running all night is not a euphoric moment that fuels you with a direct happiness to be alive. This is hippy bullshit. The reality is it will get light and you'll probably barely notice. You'll be too busy trying to lift your feet and not be taken out by tree roots that could send you tumbling into a ditch. When dawn breaks, the likelihood is you won't even know what day it is. The happiest thing about seeing the sun rise was being able to take my head torch off and allow the dent in my forehead to fill back out.

With the sun now fully up it was easy to see the 'monsters' that filled the fields around Shortwood. As we went to climb the first stile, a gang of cows charged the fence in a way we could only take as unfriendly. I don't know who had upset them in the night but they were about as far from docile as a cow could get. We opted to take a wide berth through an adjoining field and jump a hedge to get back on track. Even then they saw us behind the hedge and decided to charge us again as we made our way quickly over the bottom stile. Safe behind the fence we childishly stuck the Vs up at them, taunting them with jokes about their mum, pies and stew. We were hilarious. That's when we realised the fence didn't look like it could withstand being charged by even a single cow let alone a gang, so we quickly ran off laughing like kids as we went.

Dropping down through Warmley Forest I was on home ground and knew we were coming up on the last stretch of the path back towards Norton Malreward. With the sun shining, the night and the start both seemed a long time ago. It was all a little surreal. Neither Jim nor I had felt the need to eat very much during the night. Possibly because starting a run in the evening meant we had already been grazing all day, so we just weren't that hungry to begin with.

Leaving the last checkpoint at Keynsham we knew we only had around six miles left to run. It really was the home straight. Despite running all night, staying awake had been fine until I tried telling myself I wasn't actually tired at all. That's when I really noticed I was and somebody had attached weights to my eyelids. This was when we both started seeing things. On one shady path through some woodland we were both convinced an old log was a rabid dog. Later on, Jim was certain a rusty old animal feeder was a large angry horned ram. Hallucinations never seemed to be nice things, like cake or kittens. Only things that could harm you. Maybe that was a survival mechanism. We just decided to ignore anything scary we saw over the last section, dismissing it as unreal. I realised afterward that could have proved to be a dangerous tactic but luckily we survived.

Climbing up over the airfield at Norton Malreward and running back down through the churchyard to the finish was a glorious feeling. All the other finishers were still waiting at the village hall cheering us in. The sense of comradeship that had filled the same hall just over ten hours earlier was as strong now as it had been before the race. As we sat on the steps afterwards, devouring a hard-earned sausage bap and coffee, we smiled at the night that had just been. Neither of us had run through the night before, yet we had survived and even enjoyed it. It hadn't been an easy run, but taking on 45 miles never would be. Despite the lows of tiredness, we always remained confident of finishing. Jim even ended up running a course best by over an hour. From a personal perspective, it was a strong two-fingers up to my fear of the dark. It was also another rewarding affirmation of the tools I learnt for dealing with my negative thinking and highlighted once again the balance of physical and mental. While I did do *some* training for the event, it was nothing like the amount I did when I ran the daytime event the previous year. Yet I only finished around 30 minutes slower. Maybe I was better at this than I thought.

A week later (and almost two years to the day since I first entered the Green Man Ultra), I once again sat at a computer screen with my wallet at the ready. Recent successes combined with a healthy delusional optimism saw me clicking the enter button for another ultra: the epic sounding Transgrancanaria.

As the name suggested, this was a race that traversed the Spanish island of Gran Canaria, from Agaete in the north to Maspalomas in the south. As part of the Ultra-Trail World Tour series of races it was a high profile event and looked colossal. It took place in March and covered a distance of 78 miles with a total of 28,000 feet of climbing through mountains. Starting at night and with a 30 hour cut-off, it wasn't so much a step up from what I had done before but a leap. It was serious stuff but it looked fun.

In the back of my head, I justified it as being only a marathon further than I'd run previously. How hard could that be? Not very, hopefully. As usual, without much persuasion Paul also decided to enter, meaning the long hard miles of hilly training over the winter months would be less lonely. It was also one step closer towards our ultimate goal of running 100 miles. If stepping up the distance by a marathon each time was now normality (and somehow it seemed to be) then running just one marathon further again would be easy. Right?

I'm not entirely sure what happened next, perhaps the increased dosage of anti-depressants were doing too good a job, but talking to Paul a couple of weeks later about our ultimate triple-digit goal, things moved from discussion to action very quickly. Somewhere between delusion, desire and having too much spare cash, we were so confident in returning triumphant from a 78 mile jaunt in the Canarian mountains that we decided to go the whole hog and tackle 100 miles, too.

Having spoken to other runners and read plenty of blogs and race reports it was clear that Centurion Running organised the gold standard of 100 mile events in the UK. They were well-run, challenging and always well supported by great volunteers. More importantly, they also offered a fantastic belt buckle for finishers. It's a curiosity of 100 mile races that buckles rather than medals have generally become the finisher's reward. This stems from the oldest 100 mile footrace of them all, the legendary Western States Endurance Run in California, which started life as a spin-off of a horse race. Choosing a Centurion event as our first 100 miler seemed a natural choice.

Looking at the calendar for an event that fitted our schedule, we settled on the South Downs Way 100 in June. It was just three months after Transgrancanaria. Running from Winchester to Eastbourne on the South Downs Way National Trail, it followed the old routes and droveways along the chalk escarpment and ridges of the South Downs. It was a monster of a challenge, with around 13,000 feet of climbing over the course. But compared to the mountains of Gran Canaria it seemed nothing more than bumpy. It was all just numbers to me and didn't really mean anything. Having previously finished the Highland Fling, we already met the required 50 mile finisher qualifying criteria for entry so we were straight in. Within a couple of dangerous mouse clicks, 2015 had just become a very big year for running indeed. To use a phrase learnt from my all-nighter watching *Yo! MTV Raps* some years before, this shit just got real!

7. Streaky Bacon

You know what it's like: you stare at your calendar at the start of a week trying to decide which days to run, trying to slot in runs where you can and trying to motivate yourself to run when you don't always want to. How can you simplify that? By running every day, of course. Welcome to the run streak. It might sound a bit crazy if you stop to think about it for too long but when you look into it, you'll find that it's fairly common. It's not a new phenomenon at all. The undisputed king of the run streak is legendary British runner and former Olympian Ron Hill. Since 20 December 1964, Ron has run at least one mile every single day. Even hospitalisation after a car accident in 1993 didn't stop him.

Around the end of 2013, Bear and I had talked about starting a run streak in the New Year, but whereas he started I decided it would be too much of an undertaking. But as the year had gone on and Bear's streak continued, I started to question my original decision. He seemed to be fitting it in without any real trouble. Maybe it wouldn't be so difficult after all. Now and then I would think about starting up but quickly forgot about it again. Then I saw a post on Twitter by a runner, Mike Wells, who was celebrating his 1,000th streak day with a fundraising 100km run round the Peak District. It was an awesome achievement and made me reconsider starting up. It was clearly an itch that wasn't going away.

With my birthday coming up, it seemed as good a day to start as any. So the day after I turned 45 years of age I began to scratch that itch. I had no real plan, just rain or shine, race or recce, I would run at least 5km every single day. With Transgrancanaria on the horizon, I figured if nothing else it would provide a good base to my training. Running every day could only go towards helping to keep my depression at bay, too. I had been in a good state of mind for a few months now, without any further relapses. The medication was helping and I made sure to keep active. I had also learnt to keep a record of all the little positive things as they collectively formed an important part of dealing with the illness.

To begin with, fitting the runs in took some thought. Particularly on days that I wouldn't normally run, because fitting it in around other commitments would have usually stopped me. What changed was the question I asked myself. I added a positive edge to it. It changed from, "Shall I run today?" to "When can I run today?" Once my head made that adaptation, the whole thing became second nature. On days when I couldn't run during the day or evening, I would get up earlier and run around the block before everyone else woke up. Some days, when I was home alone with the kids, I had to wait until my wife came home from work late in the evening and go out for a run before bed. But I always went out.

Surprisingly it only took a couple of weeks before my body didn't feel any more tired than it normally did. By running 5km every day, you gain a base mileage of almost 22 miles a week before you've even begun to think about other training. Add in speed sessions, run commuting and long weekend runs, and it became very easy to start to build my mileage up. It was exactly what I needed.

Moving through the autumn months, my training was ticking over nicely. The streak was continuing and I ran the Two Tunnels Marathon in Bath, which has the longest underground section of any race in the UK. My time was unremarkable but as a long slow run it was good training. The streak was quickly accumulating days now and the count was approaching the magical three digits. Sunday, 21 December 2015 was to be day 100 and I wanted to celebrate it with something different. After several conversations about what this could be, I settled on running 100 laps of a running track. Not as a race but just for fun. Yes, I said 100 laps. I also said fun. It's all about the numbers.

One-hundred laps of lane one of a standard 400m running track equates to just a touch over 25 miles. Not a problem in terms of distance as I was upping my mileage anyway. However, given the time it would take, I needed to start early so that it didn't eat too much into the day. The problem was that Sunday, 21 December 2015 was also the Winter Solstice and the shortest day of the year. Kicking off at 6am meant I would be starting - and running for some of the time - in the dark. Luckily there is a great track only five minutes from my house. Even luckier was that the running club based there, Bristol & West AC, were kind enough to lend me a set of keys to let myself in to run at such a stupid hour. However, my luck didn't extend far enough to get use of the floodlights. No problem. Head torches until dawn it was. As usual I was not alone in my escapade as Paul had decided to join me in this special pre-Christmas loop-fest.

Our plan was to set up a camping table near the start line for refreshments. We would load it with flasks of coffee and cakes, then run reps of 20 laps before stopping for a quick refuel and going again. Like all the best plans, it was simple. Twenty laps worked out to be about five miles in distance, which in the realms of breaking big problems down into manageable chunks worked well. We weren't planning on running it fast and it was never about the time, it was purely about the laps. So at 6:15am, head torches on, we set off on our first chunk of 20, heads down into the wind and sideways rain.

As we set off, we laughed at the very notion of what we were doing, it was bonkers. But the novelty quickly wore off as we settled into a rhythm. Chatting away, we ticked off the first set of 20 laps and before we knew it we were stopping for our first breakfast of fruitcake. Yummy, if somewhat soggy. As we set off once again, we ran lap after lap with our conversation continuing. We covered all manner of topics from letting young kids go to the shops on their own to what we were having for Christmas dinner (lamb). The sun came up but the rain didn't abate. The hours ticked by and as the lap counting app on my watch reached the low 70s, the conversation went quiet as we worked our way towards the next cake stop.

One of the things people who don't run much want to know is what you think about when you're running long distances. And it depends on who I am running with. Even when you run with the best of friends for hours at a time, there are periods when silence is just what you need and all you want is to put your head down and get on with it. Then it becomes a game of distraction - keeping yourself mentally occupied as the miles tick by, yet continuing to dismiss and manage any negative thinking.

As a parent of young children, distraction techniques certainly aren't anything new to me. Whenever we needed to entertain the kids (aka keep them quiet) while waiting for something, such as in a restaurant, we play games. One of the most successful of these is the alphabet game. It's simple. We roll through letters, from A to Z, naming things on a chosen topic. This explains why, as I reached the mid-70s in lap count, I spent 15 minutes trying to think of a country beginning with the letter O.

I had started playing the alphabet game in my head with countries. Algeria, Belgium, China, Denmark went the thinking, ticking off multiple countries per lap. Japan, Korea, Lithuania, Macedonia, Nigeria… but then I got to the letter O and my brain froze. The trouble with running is that as you run, your brain loses the ability of clear thought. If you've ever tried to work out your splits on the move, you'll know what I mean. I honestly can't tell you how many laps I ran around that track trying to think of a country beginning with the letter O. It was certainly a lot of laps. Much like a goldfish swimming around a bowl, every lap I seemed to come up with the same ideas. For some reason the only word I could think of that began with O was 'orangutan'. And I'm pretty certain that isn't a country. The thing was, though, the game did its job. Despite my inability to recall international geography, the laps were building up nicely and we were getting closer to the magical 100 total. As we set off on our final set of 20 laps, I began to think about how I had been running for the last 100 days. Over that time, despite my initial concern about getting too tired or injured, I had found myself getting fitter and stronger every week.

We finished our 100 laps in just under four hours (minus the cake stops) by which time the sun had risen and we had polished off most of the Mr Kipling. Yet it still hadn't stopped raining. Not that it really mattered. As Bear reminded me a few days before, there was a time when running 25 miles around a 400m running track would have seemed like a bloody stupid idea. How times have changed.

Oh, and it was Oman. The country I needed was Oman. But what about the letter X?

As a training run it had been something completely different and perversely fun. It was exactly what we needed beside all the basic mileage. The monotony of looping the track was also great practise for switching off from everything and just running. I also now knew what Paul was having for Christmas dinner. It was a great confidence booster and proof the run streak was really helping to improve my fitness. But how long would I be able to keep it going?

STILL NOT BIONIC

Visiting an old friend during a training run

Paul and me happy to be in Scotland

The stunning view from the top of Conic Hill

Me, Bear, and Paul at Inversnaid

Posing at the top of Solsbury Hill

Paul scoffing pizza in his trademark Bristol Rovers top

The climb to the top of the world

The line-up at the start of the first Midnight Express (© Steve Worrallo)

Jim Smith finishing the Midnight Express in a personal best (© Steve Worrallo)

The large bling reward   One-hundred laps of the track complete

Paul was pretty tired after a mere one-hundred laps

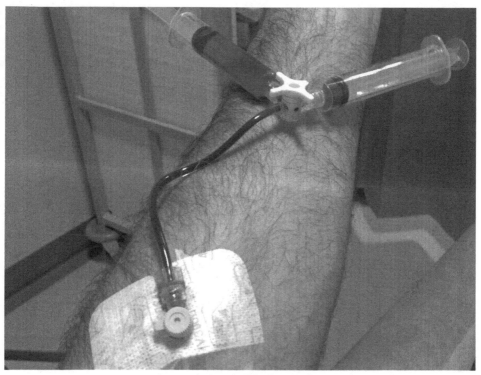

The scary looking bubble ultrasound test

With the Grand Pier closed all there was to do was run home

The creepy letter addressed to me

And then the snow came in the Chilterns

Bear went polar in the snow

Happy to finish Country to Capital in a great time

Kevin and Paul sunning themselves in Gran Canaria

The excitement of collecting race numbers from the expo

This just got real! My Transgrancanaria race number

The magical finishing line

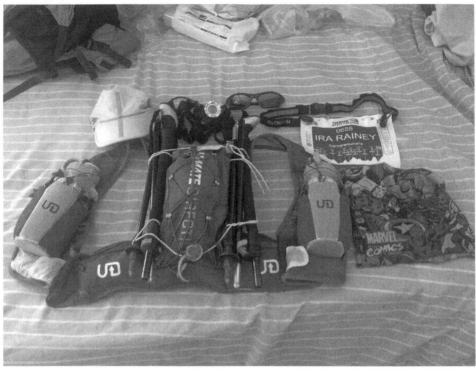

Backpack loaded for an epic adventure

Waiting nervously at Agaete for the start

Stood in the starting pack waiting to head to the mountains

The cold beer of consolation

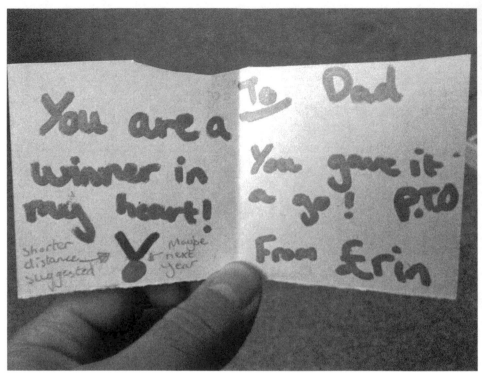

The welcome home card from my daughter

Adrian, Mark, me, and Paul on a recce run before the Midnight Express

8. Achy Breaky Heart

With the haematologist having dismissed the possibility of blood clots in my lungs, it was time to look elsewhere for answers. What could have caused my hospitalisation the year before? My tenacious GP, clearly with budget still to blow, referred me to the Bristol Heart Institute for more investigations with a consultant who specialised in sports cardiology. It sounded ideal. Even more ideal was during my consultation while once again recounting my long recent medical history we came onto the subject of running an ultramarathon around Bristol. "Oh, is that the Green Man?" asked the consultant. I was initially taken aback by his question. Most doctors I had seen would pull a painful face or shake their head at the idea of running 45 miles in one go. Yet here was one who not only didn't dismiss it as a stupid idea, but also knew of the exact race I had run. Confirming it was, he laughed: "I'm training for it at the moment. How is it?" So not only was this doctor a runner, but he also knew about and even ran ultramarathons himself. Triple ideal.

Following a discussion around the relative merits and risks of running significant mileage in training, he decided I should undergo a range of tests. The investigations would hopefully uncover two things. Firstly, did I have a congenital heart condition, such as a Patent Foramen Ovale (PFO)? A PFO is basically a hole in the heart that didn't close properly after birth. Most people never know they have one as it's usually a silent condition. The main problem comes when blood passing through such a hole contains clots. Tiny harmless clots form in our veins all the time. But if one of these clots passes from the right to the left side of the heart - such as through a PFO - it has a chance of reaching the brain. That could be catastrophic, causing a TIA or even a full-blown stroke.

Secondly, I would be tested to see if I had developed Cardiac Arrhythmia: an abnormal heart rhythm. This is a problem with the rate or rhythm of your heartbeat that can lead to the formation of clots. According to the consultant, it was also becoming increasingly evident that extreme endurance athletes can develop a thickening of the heart muscle, known as Cardiac Fibrosis. This can increase susceptibility to an irregular heart rhythm. There were a lot of big words flying around, and my confusion was compounded by me asking even more questions as we went along.

Either of the conditions I was being tested for could go towards explaining what had happened the previous year. Personally I'm always happy to undergo as many tests as I can get thrown at me. I'm very much a 'would like to know' person. I don't see the point in trying to ignore something if you think there could be a problem. It goes back to one of the lessons from the CBT. Is it a problem you can do something about? If it is, then don't ignore it.

So lined up over the coming weeks were several return visits to the institute. First was to get wired up to a mobile monitor that would record my heart activity over a 24 hour period. The box, a little bigger than a '90s mobile phone, had several long wires coming out of it that were stuck around my chest. With the exception of feeling like I was caught up in a spider's web when trying to sleep, on the whole it was unobtrusive and I forgot it was there. After returning the recorder I found myself back at the hospital being wired up to another monitor. This time for an exercise stress test. The idea behind the stress test was to determine if any abnormal heart activity occurred while I ran.

After being shown into a small windowless room tucked away at the back of the hospital, I was asked to strip to the waist. I then stood extremely still while a nurse shaved my chest. It wasn't a fetish of hers but so that the sticky sensors would stay attached. Not being much bigger than a cupboard, the room was almost filled by a treadmill, along with the two doctors and a nurse. It was definitely cosy... and pretty warm.

The test involved running on a treadmill with a slowly increasing pace until I reached my maximum heart rate. As the treadmill started up and I began to jog, I couldn't help but feel slightly embarrassed running topless while being watched by three women. Not uncomfortable, just a touch self-conscious. It wasn't a sexual thing, they were professionals, but at the same time I was acutely aware it wasn't the Diet Coke guy on the treadmill in front of them. It was definitely odd. With wires attached to my chest, a blood pressure cuff on my arm, and legs spinning on the treadmill, in my head I was re-enacting the epic opening titles of *The Six Million Dollar Man*. As I ran, I played the theme tune in my head and quietly made the bionic noises to myself. I think they thought I was doing a dolphin impression.

My training overall had continued to progress nicely and being well into the swing of my run streak I was in reasonable shape. As the treadmill speed increased, I upped my stride and kept pushing. The trouble was, my heart rate wasn't really increasing along with the pace. Puzzled faces checked the equipment was working and decided to just keep pushing the speed up. Being honest, they were more used to dealing with people who were often not that fit, and even sometimes with mobility issues. All that said, I took the fact I set a new duration record for the test as a positive. I was a sweaty topless mess come the end, but one who was a little less embarrassed by it all.

A couple of weeks later I was back again, this time for an MRI. The scan would help to determine if I had developed any scarring of the heart, or fibrosis. It was a standard affair, and I'd had enough

MRI scans over recent years to feel comfortable in the noisy enclosed magnetic space. Just don't wear a large metal belt buckle.

The final test was the rather childlike sounding bubble ultrasound. This was the one that would determine if I had a hole in my heart. To achieve this they inserted a line into a vein in my arm, drew out some blood and mixed it with a saline solution. During the mixing process, lots of tiny bubbles formed in the liquid which was then injected back into my arm while somebody else performed an ultrasound scan of my heart. The test was repeated several times and a video of the scan was taken. Lying on my side watching the screen as the scan was happening, I saw the frothy solution enter the right-hand side of my heart. But watching, I was convinced bubbles had also appeared on the left. As the test was repeated, the same thing happened again. Was that a hole? Sitting up after the test had finished, I asked the guy performing the scan if that was what we had seen. Despite being non-committal about the results, he confirmed some of the bubbles looked like they had crossed from the right to the left. I was a little in shock. I had a million questions buzzing around in my head but couldn't formulate them into anything coherent. The bigger problem was the people performing the test weren't the ones to give me answers. For that I needed to wait for a follow up appointment with the consultant. The trouble was that was a whole month away.

One very long month and much Googling later, I was back for an appointment with the consultant. The results of all the tests had been collated and reviewed. Listening to my chest at the appointment, the sounds coming from my heart were deemed unremarkable. I guess in a way that's a good thing. Unremarkable is a word I've always felt sums up my running endeavours, so to also apply it to my health isn't exactly a surprise. It was the story of my life. After a month of dwelling on the thought I could have a hole in my heart, I was pretty keen to discuss the matter. The doctor, however, was less worried by it, starting off the conversation asking about my running. As we moved through the previous test results, everything from the monitoring, the MRI and the fitness test had come back normal. That was good to know and very reassuring.

When we got onto the subject of the bubble test, he had reviewed the video and noticed a late crossing of a couple of bubbles. The fact that there were only a couple, and that they arrived a couple of seconds after blood entered the right side of the heart, dispelled the notion of a PFO. If a hole was present, the bubbles would cross over much more quickly and in larger volumes. The nature of the discovery was more consistent with a small Pulmonary Arteriovenous Malformation (PAVM). Shit, I hadn't Googled that. Luckily he explained more. In simple terms, a PAVM describes the existence of small holes between blood vessels in your lungs. This would explain how the bubbles in the test had crossed over. The fact that only a tiny amount had made the journey indicated that any holes were likely to be very small.

On the face of it we had a possible explanation for the TIA. However, the opinion of the consultant was that the PAVM was "very, very unlikely to be the source of an embolic phenomenon causing a stroke". Talking over the dangers posed by the malformation, it was his belief it posed no significant risk. The chance of a sizable clot forming, making it through the heart, across the PAVM, and making it to my brain in one piece to cause a stroke was tiny. So small it didn't even merit the potential complications of being put back onto anti-coagulation drugs to help prevent future clotting. In short, all clear.

After spending a month investigating and worrying what treatment I would receive for a hole in the heart, I was walking away with (almost) a clean bill of health. The discharge letter I was sent following the appointment even stated the consultant would be happy for me to continue exercising and running competitively.

When he said 'competitively', I assumed he'd never seen any of my finishing times.

Having now gone down every avenue of investigation and come back out with a clean slate, we had run out of routes. It would seem that while there could be a possible cause to the TIA in the malformation, it wasn't something that anybody was worried about going forward.

It was great news. Particularly seeing as there was still the small matter of getting a medical disclaimer form signed for Transgrancanaria before I would be allowed to run. It was now only a couple of months until the mountainous run across the Spanish island. Not forgetting a mere three months later, a further 100 miles to be run on the South Downs Way. I was still carrying on my run streak and that was going well, but it was time to think about other difficult elements we could face, like running through the night. Having comfortably finished the Green Man Midnight Express back in August, I was a little less worried about running in the dark. My night demons had been shoved behind the sofa. But more experience was still needed. That's when we decided to go to the seaside.

9. Weston-super-Dark

Sometimes when you read things, they stick in your head about as well as custard in a sieve. Other times snippets linger: ideas, things that inspire you or make you think of the world differently. Several years ago, I read *Ultramarathon Man* by Dean Karnazes and loved how the book opened with Karnazes running through the Napa Valley in California at midnight. It seemed like a bonkers idea at the time, running right through the night, I mean who does that? Well Dean, obviously, but it wasn't something that I'd ever considered doing just as a training run. But why not? Clearly it was an idea that had become lodged somewhere in my normally woolly and busy head. Placed somewhere accessible enough for me to think it was a good idea and almost normal. This is how I found myself outside the Grand Pier in the seaside resort of Weston-super-Mare at midnight on a Friday night in January. I was 26 miles from my home in Bristol with no way back other than on foot.

It was clearly all Karnazes' fault in the first place. Which was why, as I sat waiting to go out for a very different Friday night than I would normally have done, I Tweeted my plan and tagged him in the post. As well as the usual sharing of my runs with the world, I also posted the Tweet because I knew doing so would force me to stick to the plan. I couldn't back down once it had been made public. Not that I wanted to but the weather outside was horrendous. The wind was blowing a gale and battering the front of the house with a torrent of driving rain. The idea of heading out and spending all night running didn't seem quite as appealing as it would if I was in

California. Almost as if he knew that was the case, Karnazes replied to my Tweet saying it sounded like a fun night. However, I'm not sure he's ever been to Weston-super-Mare in January.

I wasn't spending the night alone because, as usual, much to the annoyance of his wife, Paul was joining me. After posting the Tweet, I was also contacted by my fellow Bitton Road Runners club member and uber-talented ultrarunner Brian Robb. Always looking for an opportunity to get even more miles in, Brian was a solid runner who ran raced in times I could only dream of. Often running in old trainers and cargo shorts, with no GPS watch or overpriced backpack, he was also a perfect example of how you don't need expensive kit or swanky gadgets to excel. After seeing my message - at 9.30pm on the Friday - he thought it sounded like fun and asked if he could join us. The duo was now a trio.

An hour later and the three of us met up to run the five miles from my house to Bristol Temple Meads station to begin a night of adventure. As we ran along the River Avon towards the city, we invoked looks of confusion from ducks and dog-walkers alike. Our spirits were high for our night of adventure, despite the seriously adverse weather. We were out now and there was no going back.

After almost missing our train, dodging drunks and surviving a relatively short rail journey, we found ourselves at the seaside. At night. In winter. But as the proverb goes, fortune favours the bold. By venturing out into the worst storm for many months we discovered the weather in Weston-super-Mare was actually dry and warm. A world away from the gusty winter monsoon we had left behind in Bristol.

One of the other things I remember vividly from Karnazes' book is how he scoffed on pizza during his run. It sounded great. I love pizza, so let's find a shop I thought. The trouble was, it wasn't a wise idea to stand around in a takeaway after midnight on a Friday in Weston - especially wearing tights and a running vest. It certainly didn't take long to get into a conversation with merry folk, but unfortunately not a conversation you wanted to be having. The pizza plan was shelved and I decided to stick with the handful of jaffa cakes stashed in my backpack. Brian was sorted, too. He had a triple pack of chicken slices in his trusty Tesco carrier bag.

Once we started running, it became apparent we were all overdressed for the unseasonably warm weather. We needed to stop more than once to strip off layers, to looks of even more confusion from passing drunks and police cars alike. Heading away from the city, we followed the rural A370 in the direction of the distant orange glow of Bristol. Despite being a main road, it was dark, but both mine and Brian's torches were eclipsed by the car headlight Paul seemed to have strapped to his head. It was like a small window of daylight on the path in front of us. If nothing else, it allowed us to pass the time with a shadow puppet show as we ran. Note to self: new head torch needed.

Running through the night is very different to taking on the same course during daylight hours. For one, you can't really see where you're going outside the beam shining out of your head, and for two it is deathly quiet. Stopping as we did in random bus shelters for a midnight feast of jaffa cakes and chicken slices, it was somewhat eerie. There were no buses, no people and mostly no noise bar the odd owl. It was as if everyone else had simply vanished. It was creepy. To move further into the Hammer House of Horror territory, after running out of water, Brian suggested we visited a graveyard. Apparently most churches have outside taps to enable flowers to be watered. Who knew? Sure enough, after wandering around between graves somewhere around Backwell at 3:30am, we stumbled across a tap and gratefully refilled our bottles. Praise be.

By now we'd run around 18 miles away from the coast and I had been awake for even more hours. I was starting to get tired but we still had a long way to go. The novelty of running through the night had worn off long ago. I was ready for bed. Brian, of course, was bouncing along, but I was moving slowly now. Without the structure of an event around me I was finding the motivation to keep going hard. I also had a desperate hankering for a can of Coke. However, there were still three or four miles until we hit any kind of civilisation so the chance of finding anywhere selling drinks before then was extremely unlikely. I began to think I was a little underprepared.

As we reached the top of the Long Ashton bypass with the bright lights of Bristol laid out in front of us, the bad weather returned. We slowly jogged down the fortuitously closed dual carriageway into the rain in search of an all-night shop selling sugary pop. As we ran past Ashton Gate stadium, the home of Bristol City football club, lifelong Bristol Rovers supporter Paul scowled, and we plodded on towards Bedminster in south Bristol. After miles of dark country roads and with increasingly heavy eyelids, I was absolutely ready to stop. A park bench would have been very welcome for a little sleep. But then, with five miles still to go, we stumbled onto a 24-hour oasis: Asda Bedminster. Closed rural villages had given way to the edge of the city and all of a sudden we were blessed with a superstore full of choice. Including Coca Cola: vanilla, cherry, regular - you could take your pick. The thing was, by that point I was beyond caring. Mentally I was done in. I ambled around the mostly empty store in the hours before dawn, and bought a cherry-flavoured six-pack. But after cracking one open I realised I didn't even want it any more. We sat in the store for a while, preparing ourselves for the last five miles home. In my head I considered calling a taxi, or even waiting until the buses started running, but that would be giving up. As we got up and sauntered out of the store, head torches still blazing, the security guard watching the door eyed us with a mixed look of confusion and suspicion. I'm sure he really wanted to stop us to ask what we were doing, but he was busy keeping an eye on the

Goth couple pocketing bottles of vodka in the spirits aisle.

Leaving the store behind, we shuffled along the Feeder Canal heading for home. It was a slow plod at the very best. After having already run five miles to the station and then a further 23 to Asda, jogging the last few seemed pretty irrelevant. We were close enough now to know we would finish even if we were moving at slower than walking pace.

I put the key in my front door at just after 5:20am after leaving the house the day before. It was fair to say I was exhausted, but I didn't have much time to sleep. Even after the night of running, I was planning on popping along to my local parkrun to adding a further three miles to the tally. Yeah, it sounded a bit crazy but then again I'd just run 30 miles through the night - how much more bonkers could it get? After two hours of sleep, I got up, drove to Pomphrey Hill and ran a further 5km. It was very slow but it fulfilled my crazy idea of running through the night. It also gave me the opportunity to destroy a bacon roll as I waited for the rest of the finishers. Paul stayed home tucked up in bed but Brian also added the parkrun to his night of running. But whereas my legs barely shuffled me around, Brian's time was of course unaffected by his lack of sleep and preceding miles.

As a training session, running home from the coast at midnight had certainly been different. It ticked all the boxes of running through the night when tired and keeping your head together. But only just. It certainly hadn't gone as smoothly as the Midnight Express had, but maybe that was a good thing. It made me realise I couldn't be blasé about it all and that some runs were going to be mental battles. With just eight weeks to go until we flew out to Gran Canaria, it was exactly what I had needed. I had one race left in my training calendar before flying out to the Spanish mountains. A positive result there would give me a much-needed boost in confidence.

STILL NOT BIONIC

10. Chalfont and Latimer

Is Chalfont and Latimer station located in Siberia? That was the question I asked myself as we sat with the doors open for what seemed like an unnecessary length of time. I didn't have a thermometer to hand but I'll bet it was somewhere around -20 degrees. I wasn't interested in what lies the BBC weather app was telling me, it was cold. Is Chalfont and Latimer even a real place? That was another question running through my head. It seemed like we'd been on the train forever and were getting nowhere fast. When I say 'we', I was with my running companion Bear Schlenker. We were on our way to Stoke Mandeville station and our hotel for the night. On the map the hotel looked to be a very short walk from the station. But that turned out to be bullshit, Google Maps tells lies. It didn't bother to tell us the only way to walk there was down the darkest road in the world. We even passed World's End Lane on the way. It was an omen if ever there was one.

It was Friday, 16 January 2015. We had travelled from Bath to somewhere north of London to enable us to do nothing more complicated than run all the way back to London. It wasn't an entirely random location for the start of a run, although that argument could hold water. We were going to be running Country to Capital, a 43-mile ultramarathon that takes runners from Wendover to Paddington. I'd heard good things about the race, particularly the fruitcake. I like cake and I like fruitcake even more. So what better way to spend a Saturday in January than plodding my way back to London eating lots of it?

After checking into our hotel we made our way up to our room, ditched our bags and headed back down to the bar for some dinner. "Look, there's a letter here addressed to you," said Bear. I looked. He wasn't lying. Sure enough, on the desk was a letter that had been posted to the hotel yet addressed to me. That was a bit creepy. I was scared. As I gingerly opened it, inside was another envelope with my name handwritten on it. Next to my name was a hand-drawn magic wand with a twinkly star next to it. The envelope was then sealed with a wax stamp. This had now gone past odd and was veering into disturbing. Here we were in a small hotel, in the middle of nowhere – quite literally past the end of the world - and there was a letter for me. It was all a bit sinister.

I wondered if, when I opened the envelope, a finger might fall out or the lights go off and a floating pig appear at the window. I began to shake. We looked at each other giggling in fear but desperate to know what lay inside the handwritten envelope. I cautiously opened it and slid out a letter, a postcard and yet another envelope. My mind was whizzing with possibilities. Bear stood behind me at enough of a distance to not get hit with the Anthrax as I opened the final envelope. Slowly and carefully I unfolded the letter and read the note inside. It was one of those moments when you don't fully take in what is in front of you. I had to read it about three times before I properly understood it. There was no finger, there was no deadly poison. Inside was a note from Danielle. I didn't know anybody called Danielle but, reading on, apparently this particular one worked in the Magic Making Department at LateRooms.com with whom we had booked the hotel. By now I was more confused than scared. It turned out that they had written to me thanking me for booking through them. By way of a thank you, I had been sent £100 in vouchers for a running shop together with a good luck message. It was more than I had paid for the room. At face value it was a nice gesture, although thinking about it I hadn't actually told them I was there to run a race. It was touching but in a creepy stalker kind of way.

Once our nerves had settled, we made our way down to the restaurant for our customary pre-race steak and chips. In the bar we met up with fellow runners and the very people who put me onto the hotel in the first place, Phil Hall and Simon Welch. Over dinner we talked about the upcoming race as well as others, including the South Downs Way 100, which they were both also running. Food sorted we headed back up to our room to grab an early night ready for the run in the morning. It had been an exciting night for two little boys away from home. Tomorrow we were going to London.

After a reasonable night's sleep, we got up and waited for breakfast to be delivered to our room as we were promised it would be. As I was pulling on my tights and thermal base layer ready for the day, I spotted a framed poem on the wall. I had missed it in all the excitement the night before. It was a copy of *If* by Rudyard Kipling. It's a poem I knew a little of but not much. I stood there momentarily and skimmed over it until I came to the last section which talked of becoming a 'Man' through sixty seconds of distance running. Unless there was a poem written about plodding along a bland industrial canal almost being attacked by swans, there couldn't have been a more apt thought for the day. I smiled at the relevance of it. We were certainly going to be running for more than sixty seconds, I was looking forward to becoming a Man. A real Man with a capital M. Nice.

After some time, and realising breakfast wasn't coming, we made our way down to the bar to scavenge whatever was left. A couple of Weetabix and some cold toast later, we found ourselves taking a taxi ride to the Shoulder of Mutton pub in Wendover where the race started. We registered, collected our race numbers and timing chips, and loaded our bags onto the van for the finish. There were a few hundred people milling around in the car park, all trying to decide how warm or cold it was going to be. The outlook was for heavy snow. Yet as I looked up into the clear blue expanse, it seemed that once again the forecast was at complete odds with the sky.

After a short race briefing, the 300 or so runners blasted out of the car park and swarmed towards a single small kissing gate at the bottom of Wendover High Street. Bear and I ambled down at the back, not really bothered about getting there first. It was going to be a long day and we weren't in that much of a hurry. The first half of the race ran through the scenic Chiltern Hills, which to be honest I always thought were around Malvern. That just shows how much attention I paid during my Geography O-Level. It was a mix of woodland trails and little villages, which slowly passed by as we ran. The first half an hour or so was very pleasant, like a gentle jog in the countryside. Then the weather changed. The forecast hadn't been wrong after all.

The snow came and it came with a vengeance. Within a few short minutes we went from no snow to near blizzard conditions. The snowflakes were huge. It was as if somebody had left the washing machine on and the bubbles had filled their house and escaped out of the chimney. We ran on for a few miles with the snow coming down but then, almost as abruptly as it had arrived, it stopped and vanished. By the time we reached the second checkpoint the sun was back out and the day was warming up. We ditched our jackets and donned our shades. I also tucked into a very healthy portion of juicy fruitcake. Normally I struggle to eat much at race checkpoints and it was something I was working on. The secret it seemed was a good fruitcake.

Leaving the cake and the Chilterns behind, we moved on. Making our way over the M25 we had a sense of getting closer to the big city. We were heading for the industrial heritage of the Grand Union Canal. You might think that canals are long and straight beasts but that is a complete fallacy. Lucky really, otherwise it would have been even more boring than it was. To be fair, it wasn't a completely dull route and the benefit of following the canal meant it was very difficult to get lost. I guess it's just the flat repetitive nature of it that makes it slightly less interesting than a wooded trail. Still, flat meant for a much better pace.

Earlier in the week we had decided we would expect to run something around the nine or ten hour mark. This was based on nothing short of guesswork. We felt in reasonable shape with both of us still carrying on our run streak, but we weren't in any kind of position to be knocking out a prize-winning performance. For me it was more of a training run anyway (how bonkers does that sound - when 43 miles had become a training run?). It was all about seeing where my fitness was at and how I felt afterwards. Would I be able to get up the next day and keep on running, day after day? If I couldn't run well on a flat course like this, then the mountains of Gran Canaria would be even more of a worry than they already were.

Ticking off checkpoints as we ran down the canal, we hit the one turning point onto the Paddington spur of the canal. We took a left turn and carried on in the direction of Little Venice. This section of canal was even more derelict in places and the mud was so thick it was like being back in the woods. Unlike squirrels and mice, however, the only wildlife we had to endure were several groups of drunks and a national conference of swans. There were hundreds of them (swans not drunks), all just sat around beside the water. Now I'm an animal lover, but as I ran through the bevy of birds all I could think about was how they are supposed to be able to break a man's arm. It's probably a myth but I wasn't taking any chances. Ready for any attack, I ran through on heightened alert ready to thump any swan thinking they were a bit tasty. I wasn't sure if punching a swan in the face could be counted as treason, but at that point I was willing to take a risk. Luckily for them - and me - none of them moved.

They obviously saw my fists clenched.

Not really knowing the area I had no concept of where we were. After several miles, one section of canal seemed much the same as the next. One thing I did learn about canals is that the people who live on them seem to be forever fixing up their barges. The amount of people I saw sanding, painting or drilling a long boat made me wonder just how sturdy they were. Possibly not a great choice for housing.

It was when I started to see red buses crossing bridges that I realised we must be somewhere inside London, but with no signposts on the canal I wasn't sure exactly where. We ran on through checkpoints four and five, and with just six miles left we picked up our pace and headed for the bright lights of Paddington.

Without knowing exactly how far it was (the official race distance varied from 42 to 45 miles depending on what you read) we broke up the run. We took the approach of trying to run a mile before walking briskly for a minute. The variety of pace made the latter miles just that bit easier. Much to our surprise, our pace for the day had been quicker than we had anticipated. We were not on for a 10 hour time, nor a nine. Thanks to some quick super maths calculations by Bear, we realised we could run a sub-eight hour time. That wasn't something we had even thought possible, let alone factored for.

With the distance left ticking down quickly, we soon found ourselves running through blocks of flats towards the finish. People lined the canal and stood on bridges cheering us on. The miles climbed with the time. Eight hours slowly came and, with the finish still out of sight, we knew we wouldn't quite make it in such a tight time. But given it was a goal we never had in the first place, it didn't really matter. As we came around the final corner, we saw the banner across the bridge and the bright lights of the finish. It was something of a relief. In the end, we crossed the line in eight hours and three minutes. What a result! I was so excited I even forgot to stop my watch for another minute. Had we known earlier that we were that close to eight hours I'm sure we could have run a few minutes quicker. But for a goal that I always say is arbitrary anyway it wasn't important.

We collected our medals and shuffled along through Little Venice round to Paddington in search of food. Settling in a restaurant next to the station, I refuelled on burger and chips and a nice cold beer. It was dark by now, making it seem like a long day. But the run itself had passed off remarkably smoothly. With the exception of canal blindness and surly swans, I couldn't have hoped for a better final race before Transgrancanaria. Much like the 100 laps of the running track the month before, running for so many miles along a flat and quite frankly boring canal path had been an excellent test of mental endurance in dealing with monotony. Just switch your mind into distraction mode, fend off the negative thinking and keep going. Overall, training had gone well. The run streak was clearly paying dividends and my mental confidence in making my way through the mountains was at an all-time high. What could possibly go wrong?

STILL NOT BIONIC

11. Sign on the Dotted Line

As with many overseas races, the Transgrancanaria organisers insisted on everyone submitting a professionally signed medical disclaimer form before they could run. The last time I had to get one of those was for the Paris Half Marathon ten years earlier. That ended up with me finding out I had a heart murmur and thinking I was going to die.

Following on from the positive results received from the Bristol Heart Institute, I confidently contacted my GP with a copy of the form. As with most things that aren't directly medical, I fully expected to have to pay a fee to get his autograph but that would be fine. What I didn't expect was for him to say he couldn't sign it. With only a handful of weeks until the deadline for submission, I needed to get it sorted quickly or I would be going to Gran Canaria and not running.

My doctor explained that on examination of the form, it was the nature of the wording itself he had an issue with. The statement requiring a doctor's signature said: "I certify that the athlete whose data contained herein is qualified to perform The North Face Transgrancanaria 2015, in the Advanced (83 km) or Transgrancanaria (125 km) races." The ambiguity of the phrase "qualified to perform" was the crux of the issue. How could a GP tell whether I was qualified? While my recent heart test results were clear and my general fitness good, he couldn't even say that I was fit enough to do the race. Not without undergoing a bunch of fitness tests. I understood his concern but I also needed a solution pretty quickly.

I contacted the event organisers to see if they could be flexible on the matter. Their initial response was to say they don't normally have any problems with entrants getting the form signed. I guess with runners coming from all over the world, such disclaimers would be standard practice for many. When dealing with the NHS, though, it wasn't as clear-cut. Pushing them a little more, they eventually agreed to accept a signed letter instead if I could get the wording right. They would accept it so long as it stated I had no physical issues that would stop me from running an ultramarathon. It had come down to the semantics of the wording. I needed to craft something that both the race organisers and my doctor would be happy with. After some wordplay, the final letter signed by my GP said: "This is to state that I know of no medical or physical reason why Ira Rainey should not undertake strenuous exercise beyond the normal risks that strenuous exercise entails and take part in an ultramarathon." Succinct and to the point.

I scanned and uploaded the letter to the entry website where the medical certificate was supposed to be and waited. And waited. Over the next couple of hours I refreshed the page nervously every few minutes. Eventually a green button appeared on the screen. I was ready to run… well, from an administrative perspective anyway. I thanked my GP profusely and happily paid the measly £10 administration fee he apologetically asked for. A gentleman and a legend.

Everything was looking up. My form was signed, training had been going well and my health was holding up. But nothing lasts forever. This time it was my teeth that decided to mess with my plans. It's fair to say my teeth aren't in the best of shape. I have my fair share of fillings and even a couple of crowns. But as we reached the end of January 2015, my upper right six had decided to call time.

It started as a dull ache but quickly turned into an unbearable pain across my whole jaw. I've experienced pain before but this brought a whole new definition to discomfort. I took as many painkillers as was safe and made an emergency appointment with the dentist in the desperate hope he could resolve it quickly. I still hadn't run that day and as I paced aimlessly around my house not knowing what to do with myself, the last thing I felt like doing was putting on my trainers and going out for a 5km run. As I sat watching the seconds pass slowly on the clock waiting for my appointment, I had to accept that my run streak of four-and-a-half months was probably over. As important as it was to keep it going, I just couldn't face it.

Much to my dismay, at my appointment the dentist couldn't find the cause of the pain and sent me home untreated. It's known as 'referred pain' apparently. While there was clearly a problem, he couldn't find it. The teeth that were hurting all looked fine. It was only after I spent a long night in even more pain, that I thought I knew which tooth was actually causing the issue and went back the next morning determined on a resolution. Several x-rays and one swift extraction later, and the pain was finally gone.

Some 139 days had passed since I began running every day and I was gutted to see it end but it was over. Missing one day had to mean the end. That was the rule. It had to be continuous. I couldn't just carry on the next day as if nothing had happened. But on the positive side, the whole thing had improved my fitness and helped my training through the winter months. In all honesty, part of me was secretly relieved. I'd tried it, had to stop and now it was time to move on. Next stop, Gran Canaria.

STILL NOT BIONIC

12. Maspalomas or Bust

The Spanish island of Gran Canaria, nestled off the North African coast, is probably best known to many holidaymakers for sunshine, cerveza and all-day breakfasts. Under normal circumstances I'd be looking forward to spending a week heartily enjoying all three, but this trip was about running. Seventy-eight miles of running. From one end of the island to the other on mountain trails with 28,000 feet of climbing. Welcome to Transgrancanaria.

It was a Thursday afternoon at the beginning of March 2015, and the sun was shining as we walked out of the airport. With temperatures expected in the high 20s for the coming weekend, it was a jump from the single figures we had left behind in Bristol. After a cramped budget airline cabin, it was a welcome relief to stretch my legs and feel the warmth on my face. Joining me on the trip, as usual, was Paul and old friend Kevin Mowat. An experienced runner, Kev had spent the previous seven years running ultras all over the world. He took a very relaxed view on it. To him it wasn't about racing, it was about seeing how far you can push yourself. Having taken on Transgrancanaria once before, and failed, he'd decided to return for a second try.

As we sat waiting for the bus, I looked across at the mountains in the distance. They looked epic. Other than going up one in a train once in Germany, I had no experience with mountains. All I could think about was the *Father Ted* cow analogy: "These are small... but those out there are far away. Small... far away." These mountains were definitely far away but they still looked huge.

When I entered the race I expected it to be tough, but in my head I thought of it as just a marathon further than the Highland Fling. As a runner it seemed like natural progression. The route took things to another level though, with a total elevation gain almost four times that of the Fling. The problem being, while that sounded a lot, I had no real context. I'm not great with context, particularly when it comes to numbers. They jump about in front of me like disco dyscalculia. I can see them but I can't focus on what they mean or apply any sense of relevance. I could tell people it was the equivalent amount of climbing as scaling Mount Everest because that was a clear fact, but I hadn't been up Everest so it still didn't mean much. Looking at the race profile I could see the climbs weren't gradual either. I knew there would be a lot of up, but until I saw the mountains in the distance - one day before the race - I really didn't appreciate quite how much up there would be.

Travelling to our accommodation only drilled home further the scale of the challenge we had signed up to. Everybody I spoke to before the race had used the same word to describe it: brutal. The reality of the word was only now sinking in. I was excited and scared at the same time. While I was nervous about what was to come, I was also confident. I'd trained hard through day and night, was well prepared and felt mentally ready.

We checked into our apartment and took a stroll to the exposition centre to collect our numbers. Picking up race numbers is always an exciting part of an event. It's the junction between possibility and reality. Once you have the number in your possession, the only thing stopping you from reaching the glory of the finish is your own endurance. Mental as well as physical.

Outside the centre the finish arch had already been erected. There were banks of seats flanking each side and a large digital clock above it. It looked serious. We walked over and imagined how we might feel when we crossed it after traversing the island. Knackered was the consensus. Paul and I were planning on running the race together. Our 'A' goal was to complete it in around 24 hours. Our backup plan was simply survival. There was a 30 hour cut-off, which we figured would be ample. We'd already run 53 miles in 13 hours, so even generously adding on two hours for the first 50 miles would still leave us with 15 hours to run the remaining 28. When you put it like that it sounded easy.

After collecting our numbers we milled about not really wanting to do anything that consumed energy. We went for a pizza and nursed a single beer before heading back to our apartment for an early night. The race started the next day at 11pm, making Friday little more than a day of snacking and snoozing before getting a coach to the start. With nothing much to do, we lay in and got up late on Friday. It was an odd day. There was an air of anticipation and dread following us around. Here we were with nothing on the agenda for an entire day yet all we could really do was lie around like sulky teenagers. The furthest we travelled was from our room down to the on-site bar for more pizza and back again. It was all of 50 metres.

By early afternoon the nerves had kicked in. Preparing and packing our kit for the run had made it real. It was just hours away and we were itching to get going. The buses left Maspalomas for the start at 8pm so, with plenty of time to amble down, we picked up our backpacks and made our way to the bus stop. We sat around outside the locked building, killing time, sipping water and generally nodding at other runners as they arrived.

Right on time a fleet of buses duly arrived and lined up ready for everybody to board. But before anybody could get on there was a discussion between the race official and the driver. The official then turned to the assembled crowd and announced we all needed to stow our backpacks and hiking poles in the hold below the coach. Most runners had poles strapped to their bags ready to help them on the steep climbs, both up and down. The trouble was they were sharp. Muttering and swearing in a myriad of languages followed, with the consensus being a firm 'no'. Every runner had their carefully packed food and kit crammed into their bag, and nobody wanted them bouncing around the bottom of a coach. So the driver simply closed the doors. The following ten minutes saw several arguments, heated pleas and broken Spanish discussions to which the answer remained unchanged and the driver resolute. Some runners attempted to board a different coach but the message there was the same. We were at an impasse.

Standing around next to a locked coach with several hundred other runners there was a pack mentality. Nobody wanted to budge and, despite not speaking the language of most of the people around me, there was a sense of solidarity. Five minutes later, however, it became clear the driver was not backing down. The idea of a pole spike causing havoc with his upholstery obviously bothered him much more than several hundred irate runners. Eventually a single runner walked over to the coach, deposited his bag in the hold and walked up to the door. The official nodded to the driver and, as if powered by the presence of a single bag, the door opened. As the runner climbed the steps and took his seat the crowd sensed they only had one choice. One by one we placed our bags in the bottom and boarded the coach. Some things are important, others a matter of principle but, along with many of the protesting runners that night, I realised it probably wasn't the most important battle I was going to face over the next 30 hours. Let it go.

Following the road around the edge of the island, the coach took just over an hour to reach the small coastal town of Agaete in the northwest corner. This was where the race started. As everybody got off the bus, they dug carefully through the pile of backpacks stacked in the hold, making sure they took their own. Starting any race without your carefully selected kit would be bad news, starting this one without your own stuff would be a disaster. On a long run you always need to ensure you refuel on the move, so making sure you have your personal selection of tried and tested snacks and gels close to hand is important. As a known quantity it provides a foundation of confidence for a race. On shorter races you could get by with food provided at checkpoints, but on something this tough that could be dangerous. Finding out you had somebody else's bag could ruin a race before it had even really begun.

With buses still arriving, and almost an hour-and-a-half until the start, we wandered around looking for a place to shelter. While it was still relatively warm, being by the sea saw a cool breeze blowing in. I sat on a wall watching the crowds of runners filling the narrow whitewashed streets. You could see nerves in the eyes of many. The idea of running for up to 30 hours, up and down mountains, through night and day and with the heat of the Canarian sun to contend with was enough to make anyone question themselves.

As we approached the starting time, the town took on a carnival atmosphere. Large colourful projections shone onto the cliffs in the bay, drumming bands beat out loud infectious rhythms, and crowds of cheering supporters made certain nobody was sleeping. The streets were lined several people deep, all out to watch 608 runners vanish into the darkness. It was exciting. Standing at the back of the crowd, behind the starting gantry, Paul and I looked at each other and nodded an unspoken "let's do this". It had to be unspoken as we couldn't hear anything above the Spanish rapper on the PA busting out rhymes we didn't understand. Something about Gran Canaria was all I caught. But it wasn't important. Whatever thoughts or worries were rattling around in my head, they were now irrelevant. Seventy-eight miles lay between me and a cold beer. It was time to go.

As the clock struck 11pm, an air horn sounded and the horde of runners made their way out of town towards the trail. The first short road section was fast moving, but within half a mile we were already on a dusty track and climbing slowly. Being a mountain race, seeing so many runners at the start with hiking poles wasn't a surprise, but seeing how early they had them out was. Within the first mile, almost everyone around me was using them. I was planning on saving mine for the real climbs, but thinking they all knew something I didn't I took mine from my backpack and deployed them ready for action. Out of town and away from any lights it was extremely dark. The path we were on was very narrow, and the train of runners moving along it kept everyone moving at a constant pace, almost dragging everyone along. While I couldn't see what the path ahead had in store, I could tell from the chain of red and white head torch lights slowly moving up the mountain ahead of me that it certainly wasn't flat. Through the darkness, it wasn't possible to make out the peak of the climb against the sky, but seeing the torches rising and fading away into the night sky above was an alarming sight. Suddenly the elevation wasn't just a number on a piece of paper or a computer screen, it was in front of me and it was, as I had been warned, brutal.

As adults, that feeling of absolutely not wanting to be somewhere isn't one we often have to contend with, mostly as we try not to allow ourselves to end up there in the first place. But after only a few miles, the pit of my stomach was already telling me it was uneasy about the whole thing. All the previous talk and bravado was irrelevant now I was actually here… and I wasn't entirely sure I liked it. I needed to keep one step ahead of my negative thinking or this was going to be a very short event.

The first checkpoint at Tamadaba was only six miles into the race, but it was also just over 4,000 feet up. Under our loose 24-hour finishing plan, Paul and I had planned on arriving at around one hour and 45 minutes. When I looked at my watch, however, and noticed it had taken an hour just to cover the first three miles, the reality of our target already looked laughable. It wasn't like we were standing still. We were moving as fast as we could but our lungs were bursting with the climbs. It was dark, the ground underfoot was very technical, with lots of sharp rocky outcrops, loose scree, and very narrow sections that had clearly been hastily repaired. As I passed by a warning sign telling me to beware the loose footing, I made the mistake of looking to my left. There was nothing there. While darkness can hide many things, it couldn't disguise the fact that to the side of the track was a sheer drop. In the distance below all I could make out were the faint lights of the town we had left behind. The climb seemed to go up forever with lots of false promises of being at the top. Every time it seemed to level out, it switched back the opposite way and went up again.

Reaching the checkpoint at Tamadaba 30 minutes behind schedule only highlighted how much we had underestimated the climbing. We were still well inside the cut-off so refilled our bottles, munched on a few snacks and headed off into the woods. At the top of the mountain we found ourselves in the Tamadaba Natural Park, which as well as being a protected area was also the largest pine forest in Gran Canaria. The soft, wide, needle-laden trail was a welcome respite after the rocky goat trail that had brought us to the summit. After a couple of hours power hiking, it was glorious to be able to run again. In an instant our outlook changed. We smiled as we ran: this was fun. Unfortunately the reprise didn't last long.

The descent down to the second checkpoint at Tirma took us back onto another narrow zig-zagging path for almost five miles. The turns were tight, and the trail was dusty and rocky. The poles that had proved invaluable to push on coming up, were now being used for stability going down. One missed footing or badly placed pole could spell disaster. The rocks were sharp. On our way down we passed one runner being carried back up covered in blood. His race was over. The idea of being able to run the downhill sections was proving a nonsense.

After a while the descent began to level out, and moving in and around the side of a hill, we followed the trail down and back up a number of small gullies. The course marking was good, with reflective red and white tape tied to trees and rocks throughout. As we jogged along, Paul and I joked about the absurdity of it all. Our spirits were high and although progress was slow, it was steady. There weren't many other runners around us. We weren't catching anyone and nobody was close behind. It was just the two of us, the marker tape and our head torches.

Sometimes the tape wasn't obvious. One piece was tied to a tree ahead of us but we couldn't initially work out how to reach it. Between us and the tree was a ravine, around 20 feet deep and even further across. There was no bridge and jumping it wasn't an option. But looking down we spotted two ropes decorated with a bow of red and white tape. The route was down. As I abseiled a rock face without a harness, in the middle of the night, on a volcanic Spanish island, the reality of what we were actually doing struck home. This was nuts. I wasn't even sure it was nuts in a good way. Laughable perhaps, but in a maniacal sense as opposed to a humorous one. While I like to challenge and push my boundaries, over fewer than ten miles this race had taken my comfort zone and mopped the toilet floor with it.

After attempting to run downhill for almost four miles, we now had to make our way back up a short incline to a small rural farmhouse, to the second checkpoint at Tirma. We were now 11 miles in - a distance that had taken us more than four hours to reach. The 24 hour goal we started with had withered to nothing more than a dream. Thirty hours was still viable but the race was fast becoming about survival.

Standing around snacking at the checkpoint while our bottles were filled, I heard a familiar voice. It was Kev. Having gone off at the start running his own race, we had now caught him. But he wasn't in a good way. Physically he was tired but mentally he was exhausted. The sharp descents had also proved a challenge and after twisting his ankle three times he opted for self-preservation and made the decision to stop. For a second time the island had beaten him and he was out. I was gutted for him. The sole purpose of his return trip was to lay to rest the demon of the last did not finish (DNF). Instead he had merely compounded it. At that point the thought flashed through my head of quitting, too. I figured if an experienced runner like Kev had pulled out at only 11 miles, then surely there was no shame in me doing the same? But before I could vocalise my negative thinking, Paul was already ushering me on. Leaving Kev behind, we headed on towards Artenara and the next checkpoint. At just over 20 miles, it was nine long miles away and with a climb almost as long and steep as the first one out of Agaete. Joy. With most of the ascent coming in the first half of the course, progress was proving very tough. We knew we were laying the foundations for an easier run later on but that was little consolation right now.

Moving slowly up the next hill we found ourselves disappearing into a forest and running along another windy ridge. Occasionally we would come across a runner sat on a rock or a log in the middle of the woods looking broken. Mentally as well as physically, people all around us were taking a beating. Our own pace was slow now and we knew to stand any chance of keeping under the cut-offs we needed to keep pushing on without any hesitation.

After five hours of moving, and still yet to see daylight, we stumbled across a sign stuck on a post beside the trail: '105km to Maspalomas'. Shit! It seemed like we'd been in the mountains forever, yet we still had 65 miles to go. It was yet another reality check of how much the day was still to unfold. Conversation between us was scant now. In my head, no matter how I tried to battle it, the negativity was edging in and I was questioning how much further I could go. I didn't know what Paul was thinking, and for the sake of keeping each other going it was probably better that way. Keeping our demons under wraps meant they couldn't feed off each other.

Something important I learnt when dealing with depression is the tipping point between a positive state and a negative one isn't always triggered by major actions or events. Often lots of tiny issues drip into a slowly filling cup creating increasing pressure. When that cup is already on the brink of being full, it only takes a single drip to cause the cup to overflow and break you. As Paul and I continued along the trail, a combination of issues were running through my head. We were fit and we had trained, but the climbs were so much tougher than we could ever have imagined. Because of this our pace was slower than we expected and, in truth, I really wasn't enjoying it. My cup was filling.

An hour and a half after passing the 105km sign, we rounded a bend and saw another: '100km to Maspalomas'. It was like taking a hard slap in the face. While it seemed the sign could have been in the wrong place, the realisation the last one was only three miles ago was insane. After everything else, it was the final drip.

Paul and I looked at each other and despite all the reasoning in the world, deep down we knew we were done. We were moving so slowly that making the upcoming cut-offs was going to be increasingly difficult. Physically we were exhausted but still in one piece. But mentally we were broken. Nothing from my CBT training was able to address how much I wanted to stop. The negativity filling my head was untouchable.

Making the call to drop out of any race is always a tough decision but so much had built up to this event. All the training, the talk and swagger of the challenge, and it would all come crashing down at our feet if we stopped here. I knew people were tracking our progress and seeing us stop would mean we would have to explain why. We would have to justify ourselves. But I could handle the judgement of others. While there is often a twisted sense of embarrassment at not finishing a race, you can't ever continue something purely because of what somebody else might think of you. It's not the playground. Nobody can judge you or try to understand what is going on inside your head when you make that call. Even if they did and they thought less of you, then that's their problem. If you want to stop, the only person you ever have to justify your decision to is yourself. But often we are our own worst critics. All of that was moot at that point though. Regardless of how we felt, there were still four miles to go to reach the next checkpoint. We had little choice but to keep moving.

Finally dropping down from the mountain onto a Tarmac road on the outskirts of Artenara, dawn was breaking and you could already feel the temperature begin to rise. Just as when I had run the Midnight Express, seeing the sun come up after running all night didn't do anything to lift my spirits. I was well past that. Entering town at 7:15am, we were only 15 minutes inside the cut-off and close to being pulled out of the race. Although it was almost 24 hours away, we knew the likelihood of reaching Maspalomas before the 5am deadline was slim. We deliberated a little, wondering if we could carry on a bit further, but we were far enough back and moving slow enough to think we were going to get timed out at some point. Better to drop out now and live to fight another day was the reasoning. It was another case of knowing which battles to pick.

Walking into the checkpoint we announced to the race officials that we were retiring from the race. Despite some language issues, they got the point when we took off our numbers and slumped into a hard plastic chair. Across the road from the checkpoint was a small hall where a dozen or so other runners lay in various states of misery and pain. We were instructed to wait there for a minibus that would take us halfway down the island to Garañón. From there we would switch onto a second bus that would take us back to Maspalomas.

As we waited for the bus I looked around at my fellow runners. Everyone looked in a much worse state than we did. It made me feel a bit of a fraud. One guy had dried blood all down his legs after a nasty encounter with some jagged rocks. Others looked fragile and crestfallen. While we were just slow and didn't want to carry on. Sitting there I couldn't help but feel slightly disappointed at myself. I had looked forward to this race and the challenge it presented, but now I was here and because it was a bit tough I had stepped off. It had been my choice to stop, and I knew it was the right decision, but I was taking the easy option.

I sent my wife a text telling her we had dropped out. Her first comment was the slightly peeved: "You still have three days before you come home - are you sure you can't finish?" She didn't try to talk me out of it but did point out how much I had wanted it. "Only stop if you are certain," she added. I was certain.

Once the bus arrived, we took a long, slow, and distinctly sombre journey through an epic landscape. Seeing the mountains in the daylight made me glad I had stopped. What was I thinking? How could I possibly have tackled that beautifully vicious landscape? By lunchtime we were back at our apartment and, despite having been up all night, we salvaged the day with a few cervezas. It was a lengthy session and it was well into the early hours before we made our way up to bed and I fell asleep fully dressed.

When I woke, I looked at my phone to check the time. It was 4:40am. It was 20 hours since we had dropped out at Artenara. In that time we had sat about waiting for buses, travelled the length of the island, had a shower and spent many hours and even more Euros in the bar before sleeping it off for most of the night. As I lay there, I checked Twitter and saw a Tweet roll into my timeline from somebody I knew who had just finished. Already the time we had spent on the trail seemed a distant memory after such a full day, and yet here were runners only just finishing. My head couldn't comprehend being out there for that long.

Between the start at Agaete to where we dropped out at

Artenara, we had been on our feet for eight hours through the night covering only 21 miles. Compared to what we had set out to achieve it seemed pathetic… embarrassing, even. Adding the fact we also climbed 11,000 feet does add some perspective to it, but it still felt like a failure. I have nothing but the utmost respect for everyone who completed the race, and for anyone who even tried. Some 608 runners stood toe-to-toe on the start line, and before the cut-off had passed just 349 had finished. I was one of the ones who didn't. It was my second DNF in 15 years of running and a stark reminder that not all races are created equal.

In my head it felt like a reality check on my deluded ability as an ultrarunner. Who was I kidding that I could pull this off? While I was comfortable my decision to stop was the right one at the time, I harboured a feeling of frustration that we didn't carry on. And it was a feeling that was to grow over time.

The reality was I had failed. The only way to take any kind of positive from it was to try to frame the failure as something to learn from. But the only thing I could think of as a lesson was that I still didn't have full control over my internal monologue when things got tough. It would be so easy to put the blame at the door of the terrain or lack of relevant training, but in all honesty it was the inability of my mental capacity to see me through the difficult times that had brought the dream crashing down.

Perhaps the danger is that the more ultras you complete, the more blasé you become about the next one? Maybe I just didn't take it seriously enough. The biggest problem now was that my optimistic plan to return from Gran Canaria victorious and confidently smash 100 miles in the face was now in tatters. Surely it couldn't get any worse though. Could it?

STILL NOT BIONIC

13. Back to Life, Back to Reality

The real fallout from my failure to finish the race across Gran Canaria wasn't at first apparent. Dropping out because I was slow and not mentally strong enough to finish wasn't the same as falling off the side of a mountain or ending up in hospital with dehydration. After covering only 21 miles, my body felt fine. Especially seeing as how we spent the best part of the following three days recovering in a bar nursing our egos with cold beer and steak.

By the time I arrived home the run had already been put to the back of my mind and I had moved on. It was a form of self-protection. While I would re-tell the story many times over the coming weeks as different people asked what had happened, the misery was already filed away to be forgotten. There was the upcoming South Downs Way 100 to prepare for and the delusional optimist in me was firmly back in control.

I figured I'd take a couple of weeks break from running to recuperate. This largely meant just sitting around. Despite not completing Transgrancanaria, I slipped into my standard post-race state of celebratory eating and drinking anyway. Having not returned as triumphant as I assumed I would, I wasn't quite sure how to pick things up and start planning to run 100 miles. My original thinking had been to return and just carry on. I had planned to be comfortable in the knowledge that after conquering the brutality of the Canarian mountains, the undulating chalk trails of the South

Downs Way would be a breeze. With the lack of any better idea, my default position of 'think about it later' rose to the fore, and I decided to simply ad hoc my training. I would build on the fitness I had already gained over the winter. It wasn't ideal, but I could squeeze a few long runs in on the weekends and throw in some hills at lunchtime. Sorted. Then came the conversation with my wife. Well, it started as a conversation.

It started, as these things often do, with an off-the-cuff comment. I casually mentioned my plan to disappear for the weekend to go and run an upcoming marathon. It was a big race but one I had run twice before, so it wasn't as if I was fulfilling any long-held desire to do it. I just thought it would be a good opportunity to get a long run in as part of my training. To say she didn't share my enthusiasm for the idea would be to understate it somewhat. In the 14 years we have been married, there haven't been many times we have really quarrelled. Like all relationships there have of course been altercations and disagreements over the course of time, but not a lot of really angry vein-popping arguments. This is probably because we're both laid-back individuals who generally share a common perspective on things. It also helps that neither of us are aggressive or confrontational people. Occasionally, though, something snaps and the neighbours find out about it. This time, it was five foot three of unrelenting apoplectic rage.

The touchpaper may have been lit by a last-minute marathon entry but that wasn't the tightly packed payload of incendiary explosive. That was a culmination of issues that had been quietly compacting for some time. The discussion quickly turned to my lackadaisical and inconsiderate approach to running. With a 100 mile race only 11 weeks away, she was angry at the fact I had no plan. In truth I had no thoughts on what mileage I should be doing, when I might do it or how that might fit in with everybody else. It was ridiculous. If I was a single man with no responsibilities, I wouldn't have to consider anyone else and could run whenever I liked, but I wasn't. I had a young family, a full-time job, and - for now at least - a very irate wife.

It was strongly pointed out to me that alongside my total lack of preparation I had failed to recognise one simple fact: she was working for at least half of the weekends in the run up to the race. Throw family commitments and holidays in to the mix and I would have - at best - four weekends when I was able to run at all, let alone get any long runs in. On paper it looked far from ideal. But these were just the facts, not the problem. The problem was that lately, when I took something on, I had ended up in the paradoxical situation of letting it become all-encompassing while remaining entirely casual about it. I became focussed yet unbothered. These two conflicting attitudes combined to create an often impromptu and under-planned approach to training that very quickly became thoughtless and ineffective.

While some of the problem was about the time spent out of the house 'pleasing myself', the real issue was that taking on these challenges properly required commitment. Something I wasn't giving them. She had become exasperated at my increasing habit of taking on progressively tougher challenges, becoming totally engrossed by them, yet still not taking them seriously. What was the point? Hours, days and even nights spent running could be accepted and juggled if it was all for a purpose. But if you're only pissing about, well then you're wasting everybody's time. It was a strong argument.

It took a few days for the dust to settle. During the frosty subsequent period I mulled it all over and reflected on the challenges I had recently undertaken. With a different perspective and the help of hindsight, I could see her point. Being more considerate when it came to fitting in long runs would take a little work but was relatively easy. Treating events with the respect they deserved, however, would take a change in mindset. I realised that through a fusion of growing experience and delusional optimism, I had become unafraid of the challenges I signed up for. My sense of my own ability had become distorted, which in turn removed urgency and importance from training. My result in Gran Canaria was a manifestation of that problem. On reflection, I realised she was right, so I did the right thing and I apologised.

Being honest with myself, it was clear from the position I was in that there wasn't enough time to train properly for a 100 mile footrace. Mentally I was still wounded from not managing to complete 78 miles. The thought of adding almost a marathon onto a distance I had already failed to finish made me uneasy. If I couldn't do it justice, I shouldn't be doing it at all. The only sensible choice was to cancel. I talked to Paul about my plans to drop out. While he was initially surprised, he also recognised time was short and, thinking about it, he wasn't sure he could commit enough time to it either. He also withdrew his entry. With the quick typing of an email, our plans to conquer the magical three-digit distance were over before they had even begun.

Once I'd made the decision to pull out, there was a sense of relief. It was as if a pressure had been lifted. But stupidly, it was a pressure that had been entirely self-imposed in the first place. I wasn't sure if it was a pressure I wanted again. The whole idea of running so far had flipped in my head and now seemed stupid.

With no fixtures on the horizon I didn't rush back to running. I felt a little deflated by it and wasn't sure what I wanted to do next. I always liked to have a goal on the horizon as it gave running purpose. Plus, it's always good to have an adventure to look forward to. It was also important to keep active to help manage my mood. I'd not suffered from any serious bouts of depression for a while, but had come to recognise trigger points that could nudge me that way. Running helped keep it all at bay.

When I did eventually put my trainers back on and ventured outdoors, I didn't get very far before I began to experience a pain in my left bum cheek. At first it was fairly isolated, but it quickly turned into a sharp pain that shot right down the back of my leg. The more I ran the progressively worse it got. There was nothing tender to touch and prodding lightly around the area didn't seem to do anything either. I did my normal handful of stretches and gave it a couple of days rest, but it proved annoyingly persistent. Giving up on self-diagnosis, I made an appointment with my trusty physio Dave Adler. I explained the pain to him and where it was and, when I told him of my mountain climbing exploits, he was convinced he knew what the problem was: piriformis syndrome. It sounded nasty. Nothing with 'syndrome' in the title ever sounded good.

The piriformis is a small muscle in the back of the hip that often causes issues for runners covering high-mileage. Dave explained piriformis syndrome was essentially a tightening up of the muscle by the hip that can in turn squeeze the sciatic nerve. This was likely to be why I was getting pain down the back of my leg, much like the sciatica I had suffered from a couple of years earlier. He explained that it had almost certainly been caused by all the hiking in the mountains of Gran Canaria. That would have tightened up my hip flexors. When they become ineffective, it affects the piriformis, manifesting in the pain I was getting. It looked like the mountains got me in the end.

After a bit of gentle stretching out and rubbing down, he gave it some deep massage with his thumbs and then his elbow. I nearly soiled myself with pain. I didn't know if I preferred the discomfort from the injury to the agony of the treatment. Hobbling out, Dave suggested a total rest from running, plus anti-inflammatories for a couple of weeks and stretching it twice a day. If it was feeling better in a couple of weeks, then I could chance going for a short run.

Despite following the advice to the letter and continually

stretching, the issue became frustratingly persistent. Weeks passed where I was unable to run at all. It became a constant cycle of stretching, resting, trying to run and then stopping in pain. I had a number of return visits and conversations with Dave over the next couple of months before anything started to improve. Nothing happened overnight and it wasn't until the end of June 2015 that it had cleared up enough for me to contemplate running. It had now been three months since my return from Gran Canaria, and the lack of training had taken its toll. Most of my fitness had once again faded away. Back to square one. Good job I didn't have any races lined up.

14. What Happens in the Woods...

With the summer upon us and having barely run more than a few miles a week since March, Paul gently reminded me that I had said I would run the Green Man Midnight Express with him. With the nagging injury and everything else that had happened I had pushed the idea out of my head. The race was just over eight weeks away which, considering my current physical condition and the earlier conversation with my wife, meant some careful consideration.

I had offered to run with Paul because he wasn't sure of the route, and after having run the race three times and the route itself many more, I knew it as well as anyone. There were obviously huge differences to running 45 miles around my home city than taking on 100 miles along the South Downs Way. It didn't feel as serious a challenge. But wasn't that my whole problem? I didn't want to be blasé about it, but having run the race before I did have the distinct advantage of knowing exactly what to expect. Also, importantly, I would never be more than nine miles from home. It was a very low risk return to running.

With my fitness far from its peak it would take some work to get back to a level where I could get around. But by putting a plan together, I could ensure I got the right mix of miles and recovery in over the next eight weeks. It wouldn't put me in contention for a winning place, but that would never be a reality anyway. Getting around, and more importantly finishing, would be the key. I mapped out the weeks, planned what mix of runs I was going to do when, and committed the plan to the side of the fridge. That was as good as gospel.

Along with Paul, I had talked a couple of other running friends into having a crack at it. Somehow I had convinced them that running 45 miles through the night would be fun. Adrian Grimshaw was somebody I had come to know from Pomphrey Hill parkrun and he was the captain of Emerson's Green Running Club. He'd long hankered after taking on the Green Man but hadn't quite managed to find the time to fit the training in. But he could run a solid half marathon time and, knowing the sessions he put in, I believed he was capable. It was about instilling that belief into him. Along with Adrian, I had also persuaded Mark Hoskins to enter. I'm not quite sure when or where I first met Mark, but he's the kind of person who once you meet him you never forget him. Despite hailing from the opposite side of Bristol, I'm sure I'd heard his voice carried on the wind before. It's difficult to describe Mark really. He's a bit like a '70s sitcom in real life: bearded, bold, politically incorrect, yet somehow funny and acceptable. Your gran would love him. He was also perfectly capable of completing a loop of Bristol.

Neither of them had run much further than a marathon before and they were rightly nervous at the prospect of it. But together with Paul and a couple of others we made a pact to stick together and run the whole thing as a group. They could benefit from my experience of the event and I could benefit from not being out there on my own. One of the great things about ultras is the sense of camaraderie. Because you're never running so fast that you are unable to talk, running in a pack with liked-minded people can generate a good social atmosphere. You can look out for each other, and it provides a great distraction from the actual distance, which always helps.

A week before the end of August and I was back at the Norton Malreward village hall for the start of the race. Looking around, there were yet again plenty of familiar faces. There were also a handful of people who made the point of coming over to introduce themselves and announce it was all my fault they were there. I've no idea how many people have been inspired to run an ultramarathon after reading *Fat Man to Green Man*, but the more races I went to and the more of them I met. It's always very humbling to meet people face-to-face whose lives you have changed in some small way. It isn't something I ever set out to do. I just lost a bit of weight, ran a race and wrote a few words about it all. It's a story that is actually incredibly common in the ultramarathon world. Personally I like to think of it as Remo's legacy; Remo was my friend who inspired the journey I originally set out on and wrote about in the book.

Race briefing and group photo done, at a few minutes before midnight, 30 hardy souls moved outside and stood quietly in the country lane. Race director Steve Worrallo gently whispered his countdown from ten to begin the race. But any premise of keeping local residents happy was shattered once he sounded the air horn setting us off into the darkness, all laughing like kids as we went. Running through the night had now become as comfortable as doing so through the day. It was odd to think only a year earlier I had stood on the same start line worried about venturing out into the dark. Now, with the exception of Paul, I was the person in the group who had the most experience of night-time trail running.

Following the same loop of the Community Forest Path, the familiar route didn't throw up many surprises. But even if the course was the same, no two nights out on the trail ever are. As the six of us made our way up through North Wick, we were pleasantly surprised to find the fields there weren't full of the same cluster of glowing bovine eyes as they had been the year before. This time they were mercifully empty. Either that or they all had their eyes closed. This time around, it was the toothless cider-fuelled sentry at Dundry, on the look-out for a serial fly-tipper, who caught us by surprise. "There's 20 guys with baseball bats in that hedge waiting for the bastard to come back," he cheerfully informed us. It wasn't a very large hedge. I assumed they were tightly packed. Either that or he wasn't great at counting. As we climbed around the remnants of an illegally dumped sofa, he helpfully directed us back onto the path through an overgrown hedge covering the kissing gate. "Well done lads! Keep running, yeah?"

Despite being dark and summer so far having been shabby at best, it was still a muggy 16 degrees through the night. That made for sweaty running. To make matters worse, after trying to eat a flapjack at the very first checkpoint I instantly felt queasy and pretty sure I was going to throw up. As we left the checkpoint in the direction of Ashton Court I decided to keep it to myself and just tried to breathe through it. With half of the group having never ran an ultra before, I didn't want to worry them any more than they already were. We were only seven miles in so it was still early days and I figured it would probably settle. At least I hoped it would.

After trying, and failing, to stomach various things at the next checkpoint I made the tactical decision to stick to a liquid diet of flat Coke and energy gels. On top of my day's pasta intake, I hoped it would see me through. I knew the run was likely to be challenging anyway, having only had enough time to do the minimum amount of training. It wasn't ideal but, with the demons of my Canarian failure to put to rest, I wanted to prove to myself that I had the capacity to get through it. I figured it was determination that got you to the finish: fitness just got you there quicker and I wasn't in any hurry.

Maybe it was because we weren't running overly fast, but the minimal training and constant sense of nausea didn't turn out to be much of an issue. Running as a group we kept each other going. We ran from one dark checkpoint to the next, crossing fields, traversing golf courses and tramping through woods, talking a lot of old crap and laughing as we went. Some of the sentences that came out of

Mark's mouth sounded as if they would be at home on the pages of a special cross-publication edition of *Viz*, *Razzle* and the *Daily Mail*. It was the perfect level of conversation to keep our spirits up and keep us moving through the night. The chat was fun, the pace was steady and we were enjoying ourselves.

The miles drifted by as we bantered our way through South Gloucestershire towards the final checkpoint at Keynsham. As the sun began to rise, regardless of our own small battles with stiles, electric fences and long grass, the world continued to unfold as it should. Ahead of us, the previous year's winner Brian Robb was pacing himself in for a second consecutive win. We were still a good ten miles from the finish, but with night having turned to day and confident in the knowledge we were going to finish, our mood was buoyant.

We stopped at the final checkpoint next to The Lock Keeper pub, posed for some pictures, refilled our bottles and generally hung out. With plenty of time on the clock and just one more short stretch to go we weren't in too much of a hurry. Everyone was feeling understandably tired and a bit stiff, but leaving our supporters behind we headed off on the last section back to Norton Malreward. The queasiness, much like the night, had passed. The Coke and gels held me up and, powered by a second wind, I led the group back to the village hall and the waiting sausages, medals and tea.

It was a low-key but glorious finish to a long night. My strategy of optimism and determination, coupled with a small amount of structured training, had successfully carried me through for which I was eternally grateful. It was also hugely gratifying to see the first-timers reach the end smiling. My confidence in their own abilities was vindicated as they posed proudly for photos with their new bling. The run helped me quash some irrational fears that had built up in my head, worries about my fitness and mental capability to see a distance through. Running within the support of a group of friends had also made a significant difference. The collective positivity makes a huge difference when things get tough in your own head. Safety in numbers was definitely the order of the night.

Sitting on the steps of the village hall, Paul and I slurped our tea and munched down on sausage baps. "You know what race opens for entry this morning, don't you?" I asked him. We both knew the answer. It was something we had already talked about briefly a couple of weeks earlier. "Let's do it," he replied. I smiled and nodded. Getting my phone out of my bag, I checked I had a decent 3G signal, opened the webpage and completed the form. Seconds after I tapped the submit button, the notification of a confirmation email flashed up on the screen. Entering races had never been so easy. Now we had nine months to train for unfinished business. Nine months until we stood on the start line of the South Downs Way 100.

The larger starting pack for the second Midnight Express (© Steve Worrallo)

The sun just rising as we reached the third checkpoint in Hambrook (© Annemarie Hoskins)

Hanging out at the final checkpoint in Keynsham (© Carol Aleknavicius)

Mark proudly displaying his Midnight Express finisher medal (© Annemarie Hoskins)

Paul with his bling and t-shirt after the Midnight Express (© Steve Worrallo)

A liquid refreshment after finishing the Bristol to Bath marathon

The undulating cliffs of the South West Coast Path

One of the tough early climbs up on the coast path

Don't stray from the marked path - may cause death

Halfway to London

Number ready for Country to Capital 2016

The one turning point on the Grand Union Canal

The starting pack of timelords at the Green Man Ultra 2016

Leading the ten hour group out from the mansion house (© Bridget White)

Leaving the final checkpoint at Blaise with concern over the time (© Annemarie Hoskins)

How to pace a ten hour ultra

The last train to somewhere on a Friday

The start of our nemesis - the Cotswold Way at night

Darkness is everywhere

My number and kit laid out before the SDW100 2016 #DontBeShit

2016 SDW100

YOUR "To-Do" LIST:

1. KIT CHECK
2. REGISTER
3. DROP BAGS →Behind Registration
4. RUN 100 MILES ☺

The simple instructions for the day

Paul happily wearing a Bristol City shirt for charity

Me and Paul with over ninety miles left to run (© Stuart March Photography)

The elation of finishing one-hundred miles (© Stuart March Photography)

Look! It's my finisher's buckle! (© Stuart March Photography)

The buckle of beauty

Refuelling - big breakfast style

Ultra beers in Bristol with Paul, Gareth, Jim, Robin, me, Mark and David - Cheers!

15. Racing Back to Fitness

The writer Aldous Huxley once wrote, "That men do not learn very much from the lessons of history is the most important of all the lessons of history." It's a cynical but astute observation on humanity, but one that has been proven true time and again as people repeatedly fall in to the same holes. Our brains are excellent at suppressing the negative. It's a form of survival. How many times have all of us as runners stumbled across the finish line of a race uttering the words "never again", only to enter another race within days? To not repeat the same failures, we need to be mindful of where things go wrong or can be improved upon. We need to be conscious of our shortcomings. For me, with recent history of not taking things seriously enough and a 100 mile race now back on the calendar, that meant formulating a plan. And sticking to it.

After talking to a few people about training for longer races, I settled on a six-month training schedule. The plan covered around 900 miles, encompassing hills, long miles and races. It also meant making sure it fitted around holidays, work and, of course, my wife and kids. It took a few days to draw it all out, carefully consulting the family calendar along the way. I put it in a spreadsheet, marked up with lots of different colours to show the various types of run. It looked intimidating at first, seeing so many months mapped out in glorious multicolour. But it felt positive to have a plan. I printed out two copies - one to keep on my desk at work, and one to be pinned to the fridge at home so everybody knew what was happening and when.

The schedule didn't begin until the middle of December, which was lucky seeing as, despite finishing the Midnight Express, my fitness was still a long way from where it needed to be. Increasing my mileage and getting back to running regularly before the plan kicked in was important. And part of that pre-training preparation came in the shape of a new local marathon. Using races as part of your training can be a good thing. They can be more social, and chances are you'll also push yourself harder than you would when running by yourself. The key is not to do too many, nor worry too much about your times.

On the face of it, the inaugural Bristol + Bath Marathon offered little in terms of special attraction or adventure. But with it being on my doorstep, it seemed churlish not to enter. There was no travelling involved, I would get to run with lots of people I knew and I was supporting a new event.

Starting in one city and finishing in another meant for slightly tricky logistics. So Paul and I simplified things by running the four miles from my house to the start. It made getting home from Bath afterwards much easier. We considered it a warm-up. Friends who drove past us as we made our way into town considered it lunacy. Nobody was wrong. The difference was perspective.

Living in Bristol and working in Bath, the race route wasn't too much of a surprise. It started by following the tried and tested path of the Bristol Half Marathon, weaving its way around the city centre, then up and down the Portway, before heading out along the Feeder Canal. Turning left at the end it joined the River Avon, and continued up through Hanham, before dropping down to the villages of Bitton, Swineford and Kelston. Reaching the outskirts of Bath, a short loop of Weston took the runners around the centre and eventually to the finish line in Victoria Park, overlooked by the world-famous Royal Crescent. They were all roads I had run on hundreds of times in my many years running, not to mention my daily commute. Because of that, I didn't think the race would hold any surprises. How wrong I was.

After the initial excitement of the start line and the bunched-up early few miles, the first half of the race was frankly dull. I guess the attraction to event organisers of routing runners under the Clifton Suspension Bridge is to rack up miles and simplify road closures. The trouble is it's barren. If the weather is fair, you can get a good number of people supporting about halfway up around the Sea Mills area, but other than that it's about as uninspiring as a road can get. Away from the city centre, the crowds around Bristol were patchy and lacklustre at best.

It wasn't until we climbed Conham Hill at 15 miles and arrived in Hanham that the course transformed into a heaving throng of cheering people. It was surreal. For miles there had been nobody, and here we were on the outer fringes of the city and supporters were out in force. This section of the course was also only a mile from my house, so there were plenty of friends and family on the route cheering me along, which was amazing. Although I consider myself so very far from being any kind of role model, running through my own neighbourhood I felt a glowing sense of pride. It brought a smile to my face and a power to my stride as I ran. All those people - all those children - who probably wouldn't normally watch people run, had stepped outside their front door and revelled in the spectacle of the marathon. Seeing runners of all shapes, sizes and ages pass through on their own marathon journey normalises the distance, bringing it into the possible. It's the same when the London Marathon is shown on the BBC every year: it motivates people to give it a go themselves.

A few miles later, as the crowds thinned, I looked ahead and made out the familiar figure of my old friend Jim Smith. I picked up the pace a little and shouted his name. Catching him up, we spent the next nine miles plodding along talking crap and laughing just as we had during that long night of the Midnight Express the previous year. It helped the miles drift by. Before we knew it we were rolling into the centre of Bath. Where the crowds had been scant along the Kelston Road, when we came into the last couple of miles they were back out in force. The twisting route to the finish was lined several deep with supporters. The noise was incredible. By this point, the additional four miles I had run to the start of the race didn't seem like such a great idea. But when you're in the final mile and thousands of people are cheering you on, your legs somehow keep moving.

We crossed the finish line with just over four-and-a-half hours on the clock, collected our bling and retired directly to the pub for carb reloading. It had been a good day and a good test of miles. More than anything it had been the home crowds and the company that had made the day. From friends and family cheering me on through my neck of the woods, to all the people who gave up their Sunday morning to cheer on friends and strangers alike. It had been great to see how positive an impact a smiling face and a casual high five can make when you are tired.

A few weeks later, and now into the start of December, Paul and I found ourselves at Lulworth Cove in Dorset. After a brief text conversation following Bristol + Bath, I had agreed to run the Endurance Life Dorset Coastal Trail Ultra. It seemed like a good idea at the time. Falling into the calendar just before the training plan started, and at 33 miles long, it helped in my quest to increase my endurance. The course wasn't exactly flat though, with close to 6,000 feet of climbing over the whole route. I couldn't decide if that was a lot. Once again the numbers didn't really mean anything to me, even with Gran Canaria as a benchmark. What we also didn't factor for was the weather. It's something you can never rely on for any race, but running a coastal path in December there is a good chance you won't get much of a tan. Nobody mentioned gale-force winds though.

Joining us on the race was Gareth. Self-billed on Twitter as Fat Dad Saltford, Gareth Strange was another local runner I'd met since *Fat Man to Green Man* had been published. A former track runner in his youth, he had long since replaced the spikes for beer and ended up many years later wanting to do something about that. My book had struck a chord with him and running had become his new vice. Talking to him on the drive down to Dorset, it turned out Gareth was some kind of number-crunching maths genius. A guru with figures. He was like my ginger number doppelgänger. Dorset was to be his first foray into ultrarunning.

Collecting our numbers on the Friday evening was an interesting experience as it was all done in a tent by torchlight. I'm not sure whether that was down to a power failure, saving money or just an attempt to make even registration look hard core. Registration sorted we walked over to the t-shirt collection table. "I'd go up a size lads as they're all on the small side." That presented me with a problem. I was already after an XL, which was the biggest size on offer. That'll be another t-shirt I never wore then. The other thing was, it was orange. Not only was orange far from my favourite colour but it was also the colour of the shirt given out at Transgrancanaria. Could a colour be cursed?

After registration, we met up with Paul who caught the train down after work. We sat in the pub loading up with the prerequisite steak and beer, talking about our race plan for the following day. Paul and I were planning to run together as usual, going out steady from the start. Gareth, however, was more competitive. Despite venturing into an unknown world, he was planning to go out fast and keep going. He was gunning for a time. Looking at the course I thought that was a bold move. Maybe it was a rookie one, or perhaps it just seemed reckless because it was something I never did. We would find out in the morning.

Heading back down to the start on Saturday, it was impossible to not notice the wind. The BBC was telling me it was gusting at up to 60 miles-per-hour and I had no reason to doubt they were telling the truth. It was far from ideal given the coastal nature of the race. There was nowhere to hide. The ultra event followed a figure of eight pattern making up about 27 miles, before heading back out again for the same six mile loop we started with. This meant passing back through the finish area twice before finishing. Something that can be mentally tough, especially when you're tired. Looking back, the odds were stacked against us from the beginning: a mentally tortuous route, lots of elevation, strong winds and an orange t-shirt. We were always going to be doomed.

As it had been dark when we collected our numbers the night before, we hadn't seen the first section. Seeing it now I realised that had been a benefit. The first climb was long and steep. And while it wasn't the longest or steepest we would encounter on the day, it was a good precursor of what to expect later. Hanging around at the start we also caught up with another runner we knew, in fact Gareth's neighbour, Robin Lewis. Robin was one of those annoying slim, handsome and naturally fit people who make life look easy. Despite only starting running after Gareth did, he was of course already much faster and more capable than any of us would ever be. And he worked for a great charity, too. Of course he did. He would be sickening if he wasn't so nice. Robin was also running the ultra. But it was a given he would be finished and probably home in bed by the time we rolled in.

As the runners set off, we all made our way up the first climb and to the top of the cliffs. The mood was jubilant and even though it was ridiculously windy, it was luckily an onshore wind. Had it been going in the other direction, we would have been in the sea in seconds. As Paul and I slowly plodded up the long steps, Gareth had started edging away from us. Robin was obviously already out of sight.

The South West Coast Path we were running along turned out to have all the properties of a rollercoaster. Not only was there a long queue of people, and lots of steep ups and downs, but Paul had also started to feel sick. When he turned up the night before he already sounded chesty and rough. Had it been me I would have probably sacked it off. But Paul figured since he was here he might as well give it a go. That turned out to be a bad decision. By the time we reached ten miles he started heaving and being sick. Coming suddenly it caught me off-guard and, standing so close to him, also made me retch. I wasn't sure if whatever he had was catching but the heaving certainly was. Ever supportive, I moved further away to stop myself from empathy gagging. From there on, progress was slow as we stopped roughly every mile for Paul to be sick. I suggested he pull out as we passed through the checkpoint at Lulworth Cove but he was convinced he'd be fine and wanted to keep going.

Running across the pebble beach we once again climbed to the top of the cliffs and entered a military firing range. We had been warned at the race briefing not to stray from within the yellow markers on the path as that was the only route that had been cleared of live ordnance. The sign that said: "Do not touch any military debris as it may explode and kill you" was certainly one I'd not come across in a race before. This was one trail you didn't want to have navigation issues on.

The wind was now stronger than ever. As we dropped sharply down out of the firing range and stared up at a set of steps leading to the sky, our pace was already very slow. Climbing hundreds of steps practically on our hands and knees did nothing to help that. Between Paul vomiting, the wind hampering our progress, and not feeling the love for the constant steep climbs, we took three-and-a-half hours to cover just 15 miles.

There were still people behind us and time on the clock, but it was hard going. Much like our time in Gran Canaria, for me at least, it had stopped being fun. I was battling my inner demons but not winning. While running ultra distances will always involve some form of misery, it should still be something you want to do and gain enjoyment from. It's a fine mental balance between stepping outside your comfort zone to achieving something and questioning why you are bothering at all. If you've reached the latter then you will always be fighting a losing battle. It's important to accept you will always have an internal monologue to battle, but it's knowing when to tell it to shut up and when to listen. There are no prizes for how miserable you can make yourself in the pursuance of a largely subjective goal.

As we reached the checkpoint at 16 miles, Paul listened to sense and dropped out. He sat in the marshal's car out of the wind and waited until he could get a lift back to the finish. I battled with myself to not pull out, too. Not that I was sick like he was, I'd just had enough. Stopping now would be easy, and I could kid myself that I was doing it to look after Paul. But that was a weak argument and I knew it. I didn't allow myself to take the easy option and I carried on. I was fit and healthy and had no reason to stop. The climbs were brutal and the wind was shit, but I decided to see it though. I kept moving at a slow pace and caught up with some runners who were doing the half marathon distance. They provided a helpful distraction for a while. Somebody else to talk to, to help pass the time. But after a while, as they were moving even slower than I was, I made the decision to push on by myself. I say push on, but that sounds like I was actually making progress. In honesty, I was barely moving forward at all. A combination of tiredness, despair and wind saw me scarcely shuffling, wondering what I was doing.

Battling the gales along the top of the cliffs, I looped back around the firing range and followed the steep path back down to the pebble beach at Lulworth Cove. After I trudged across the sliding shingle, I climbed the long boat ramp to the village. Ahead of me I saw the car park and, for the lucky ones, the finish line. For the not so lucky, it was simply another checkpoint. But with 27 miles of hilly windy misery behind me, the magnetic pull of stopping drew me in. My resolve folded and I dropped out. Having been running for seven hours, going back out for another six miles, in that weather and with those climbs, just wasn't happening. Had the course bypassed the finish I probably would've kept going and sobbed gently, but it was easy to stop so I did. It was another DNF but I didn't care. I just didn't care at all. I didn't want it enough. Stopping held none of the usual sense of disappointment at my performance. I was just happy it was over.

Telling the checkpoint staff of my intention to quit, I looked around and saw Gareth. It turned out, after going off like a rocket at the start and getting a good lead, he eventually slowed down. So much so that despite only bumbling along myself, by 27 miles I had caught him up. More importantly, he was of the same opinion as me - going back out for more hills and suffering wasn't on the agenda. He was out as well. Stood alongside Gareth was Robin's wife, who told us he had passed through the last checkpoint some time ago and was now heading back for the finish. Of course he was. All I could think was damn that orange t-shirt.

STILL NOT BIONIC

16. Wobble

The day after returning from Dorset, I sat in my armchair and mulled over the race and how I had felt out there on those windy cliffs. I opened my laptop and tapped out an email to Paul: "Dude, I'm seriously starting to question the merit and sanity of running 100 miles. I'm just not sure I want it enough to be able to keep going through it. Yesterday was pretty miserable. I know that was in large part because of the weather and the elevation (which after that and Gran Canaria I know I'm not fond of), but imagine what being out there four times that would be like. And for what? We always talk about the arbitrary nature of running for a fast time, but I'm not sure running an arbitrary distance just to say we've done it is any different. I just wonder if we don't get wrapped up in it all a bit too much."

It didn't take long for a response to roll back in: "Wow. I was actually enjoying it yesterday, all bar feeling ill. I knew I really shouldn't have been running anyway. I'm not even thinking about 100 miles yet as we have a good few more runs until then. Forty-five miles is a walk in the park for you now - would you have said that three years ago? We know what runs we enjoy and are comfortable with, but to keep the interest we need at least one big target, even if we fail! One-hundred miles is our big target. We must train accordingly which involves hard runs like yesterday. Remember that yesterday you ran a fucking hard marathon. You need to write another book about this next step of the running journey: doubts, fears, failures and triumphs. And remember at the end of 100 miles of pain and misery you would have run (and walked) 100 miles. Even the Proclaimers just sing about it!"

It was the straight-talking common sense I expected from Paul, and it made me stop and think about it differently. Were they serious and valid concerns, or was I just having a wobble after a bad day on the trails? We all have shit runs occasionally, but the key is to not let those be the ones to define you. It's how you get back up and learn from them that makes the difference. Being honest and talking about my thoughts had helped provide a more positive approach to my negative thinking and calm my doubts. Paul's email ended with the sort of line that can only be uttered between friends and made me smile: "Now pour a beer like me and let's get out next Sunday and have a proper chat about it. We can do this." Wise words.

The subsequent conversation eased my mind and quashed my fears sufficiently enabling me to move on. He was right. We needed to take the training seriously and treat it with respect. I was in a very different place than I had been three years earlier, and a bigger challenge was achievable with the right preparation and mindset. It's unrealistic to expect to take on any large challenge without feeling somewhat nervous about it. Looking back, that had been part of the issue with earlier races: complacency. Maybe the fact I felt uneasy about it was a good thing. Perhaps reality had finally sunk in.

With my rainbow schedule pinned visibly to the fridge it was impossible to not be reminded of the whole thing every time I walked by. In particular, the large red block at the far end of the plan, boldly labelled SDW: South Downs Way. But the difference now was that as we moved into 2016, I was well into the practise of crossing the days off as they passed.

With every run detailed, the plan started with a weekly total of just 25 miles, adding a bit each week before having a lower mileage week every fourth week for recovery. In the mix were lots of lunchtime miles with hills, some runs to work, club runs and increasingly longer slow runs on the weekend. To bolster the regular runs, I also added several back-to-back long weekends and night runs for mental endurance. Just as with Dorset, there were more races in the plan. The next would be a return trip to Country to Capital, complete with its hills, canals and gangs of swans.

Unlike the previous year, the race was relatively uneventful. It took place in January as before, but this time Paul and I stayed in a different hotel, received no scary hand-written letters and it didn't snow. The only common ground between the two races was the steak and chips we ate the night before. With an accompanying beer of course. Nursing a minor hamstring niggle, Paul decided not to run the whole 43 miles, instead retiring at about 16 miles where he would jump on a train back to Wendover. This proved to be ideal for me as he then popped up at every checkpoint to cheer me on over the last 25 miles.

The navigation of the later stage of the race is straightforward anyway, being one long canal path, but having run it the previous year it was a comfortable and familiar run. Following on from the pre-plan build up, I was feeling pretty good about my fitness, although probably not as good as I did the January before when Bear and I finished in eight hours. In the back of my mind I had a vague expectation of around nine to nine-and-a-half hours. Given everything, I would be happy with that. But with Paul popping up at each aid station, feeding me positive vibes, I pushed on towards Little Venice at a decent pace. Leaving the final checkpoint, I put my refreshments order in for the finish, donned my head torch and set out for the last six miles.

Despite being well inside London by this point, the canal still seemed to drag on forever. I put some headphones in and listened to the radio to help provide some distraction. But by the time I reached the 38 mile point I was tired and dropped to a slow amble. It was dark, it was cold and I was on my own with just BBC Radio

1Xtra to keep me company (I was trying to get down with the kids). I knew I would finish because I knew what was coming up, but I couldn't bring myself to keep running. I broke up the next few miles by walking for a quarter of a mile then running the same, which worked well for a while. But as I reached 40 miles and the point I should have switched to running, I kept walking. I was done. I mooched along for a whole mile knowing, but not caring, there were still several more miles of gloomy canal between me and the finish. It was an odd situation to be in. I wasn't interested in running and had nobody to drag me along, yet knew even then I would still finish. I just needed to get my head down and keep moving, at any pace. Eventually it was a group of runners coming up behind me who chivvied me back into a jog. They were right, we were almost there.

Passing through the final section at Ladbroke Grove I broke into a steadier pace, safe in the recognition the end was close. Despite the chilly darkness, people lined the side of the canal and bridges spanning it, cheering the runners along. Encouraging them on to the finish and their awaiting medals. Yet again, the friendly spirit of strangers was heart-warming. Even in London.

I eventually crossed the line in eight hours and 47 minutes. It was only 43 minutes slower than I had run the year before: one extra minute per mile. It was a great result and one I hadn't expected at the start. Stooping down to collect my medal, I looked back up to see Paul standing at the finish, smiling and with a four-pack of cold beer in his hand. What an absolute legend. Collecting my bag from a marshal, I hobbled around the corner and jumped straight into his warm, waiting car and we drove back to Bristol. Obviously I made sure to rehydrate myself along the way.

The success of the day had been validation not just of the first few weeks of the training plan, but also of Paul's counterargument to my earlier wobble. It hadn't quite been a walk in the park, but

I realised that races of this distance were now comfortable. The natural progression now had to be to focus purely on the time.

STILL NOT BIONIC

17. A Master of Time and Miles

At the start of March, with training progressing well, I found myself at Ashton Court in Bristol, and the start - once again - of the Green Man Ultra. But this year was different, as I was there to be a pacer or, to use the official title, a timelord. Pacers aren't something you would typically find at an ultramarathon, but with the growth of the Green Man combined with the tricky self-navigation of the route, they had proved to be very popular the previous year. Not only could they help you get around in a certain time, but they would also make sure you didn't get lost. Four timelords covered hourly times from nine hours up to the cut-off at 12. I was running the ten-hour slot. It was a role I took on after talking to the race director Steve Worrallo about running that year. It made sense. I knew the course well, and given that plenty of people running it were there because of reading *Fat Man to Green Man* in the first place, it felt like karma. It was also about giving something back to the ultrarunning community. This was my local race, and because of some words I wrote I was now inextricably linked to it.

It was amazing how things had changed in the space of just three years. In 2013 I stood on the start line of the same event, having only run a couple of miles further than a marathon once in training. Back then I had been physically fitter and slimmer than I had ever been, and yet I was still a bag of nerves. Finishing the distance that first year, I amazed myself with what I was capable of and it changed my perspective on what was possible. Now I was helping others start out on that same journey. I wasn't as fit or as slim as I had been three years earlier, but mentally I was so much stronger. With this distance, with this route in particular, I was experienced and confident. But the time was more of a concern.

At first, I didn't think too much about it. But as the day drew closer, the responsibility of getting others around a 45 mile course and finishing in ten hours become a daunting prospect. Even though I had now run the race twice in the spring, and twice in the summer, my personal best time was still only nine hours and 48 minutes. In the back of my head I thought that if I could run it in ten hours at all I'd be happy, let alone get everyone else around as well. Pacing a road race is relatively easy, as long as you're fit enough. You calculate your average pace, run and make sure your speed remains constant. Trail races, especially long ones, are a different prospect.

Firstly, you have to contend with the weather. The winter had been incredibly wet and the route was muddier than I had ever seen it. Burst riverbanks had been commonplace, making the paths alongside them far from ideal for running on. The softer the ground, the harder the going would be, and hence more tiring having to keep dragging your feet out of the mud. Secondly, the terrain was much more varied than regular Tarmac, and often with a lot more climbs. While the Community Forest Path the race followed wasn't a mountain trail, it wasn't flat either. Factoring in the time spent walking up steep climbs would also have a knock-on to the pace we would be able to attain. The bottom line was that trying to run an average pace was a waste of time. What I needed to do was to work out how long I thought it would take to get between each checkpoint by using my knowledge of the course and factoring in the conditions. If I could stick to those times, then everything should be fine.

I was also a little concerned with what people might expect from a timelord. But after talking to Steve, my remit was clear - run the

45 miles and finish as close to ten hours as possible. Nothing more, nothing less. All I could do was run my own race. Walk if I wanted to walk and run when I could run. If people stuck with me all the better, but if they dropped off the back, even if they didn't know the way, that wasn't for me to worry about. The definition of success would be if I made it to the finish line close to ten hours. Whether anybody was with me or not was almost irrelevant. It sounded heartless but that was how it had to be.

Arriving at the mansion house to collect my race number and pacer flag, I bumped into lots of familiar faces. Mark Hoskins was running, as were Jim, Gareth and Robin among others. It was like one big running party. Whenever I find myself in large social gatherings my mind spins and I find it hard to focus on what people are saying. As more and more people came up and said hello - old friends, people I didn't know, runners I'd conversed with on social media - I couldn't remember any names or put them in any kind of context. In that position I have to switch to a safety mode of: "Alright mate, how you doing?" It's friendly, yet generic and safe. Even if you've just told me your name and I've already forgotten it, I can generally wing it until I work out if and how I know you. I did that a lot that morning.

Once all the hand shaking and race briefing had been done, we assembled outside the manor house ready for the start. Even though it had only been three years since I had first run the race, it had grown massively. That first year there were just 65 of us. This time, around 250 runners were standing on the start line. The atmosphere was fantastic. With the air horn sounded we set off around the Ashton Court grounds heading towards Long Ashton. Through the first slightly uphill mile the pack started to thin out, but even by then it was clear there were around 30 runners who had pinned their hopes to me to help get them around. The pressure was on.

The first section of the route had changed in recent years thanks to a major new road being built. This meant for a slightly more convoluted path up to the first big climb at Dundry and on to the first checkpoint. I had recced it a couple of times and was comfortable with where I was going, but it did add a couple more small climbs into the first section. Ashton Court to the first checkpoint at Norton Malreward was just under nine miles, but a hilly part of the course. I had given myself one hour and 50 minutes to reach Norton and consider myself to be on track. Walking through the muddy field on the way to the top of Dundry Hill it was hard to tell, but the pace felt about right. Reaching the top, we picked up running again and carried on down through the farms of East Dundry and North Wick before arriving at the checkpoint. I looked at my watch. One hour 45 minutes. That was close. It had been a push with the climb but I was still on track. Result.

I took the decision that as I arrived at a checkpoint, I would tell everyone around me how long I was planning on staying for and then shout out again as I was about to leave. It was the only way to make sure people didn't unintentionally drop off the back. After a quick refuel, I put out the shout and my new friends and I set off on the seven miles to the next checkpoint at Keynsham. Passing through Pensford and Publow, the fields were particularly muddy and hard to gain any real traction on. It noticeably slowed our progress of which I was mindful. I had given myself one and a half hours to reach Keynsham, and while the route wasn't exceptionally hilly, it was muddy. Pushing on through the villages of Woollard and Compton Dando we reached the edge of Keynsham and firm Tarmac. With the ability to grip more, I picked up the pace slightly as we made our way through the park towards the checkpoint at The Brassmill. I looked at my watch as I entered the car park and called out my number to the marshals. Once again I was up on my projected time. We had covered the last section in only one hour and 21 minutes. While we seemed to be getting faster and gaining on the target times, I made the executive decision it would be time in the bank for later when everybody started to tire. The numbers with me had now dropped down to about 20. It would be interesting to see how long that would last.

Putting the shout out, we left the car park and set off following the path of the river. Being not far from my house, the section towards and up through Warmley Forest is one of the most familiar bits to me. Unfortunately it is also one of the longest parts with 12 miles between Keynsham and the third checkpoint at Hambrook. I had allowed two hours and 40 minutes for this next bit. While the climb up through Shortwood isn't insignificant, there aren't many other big hills to contend with. It's just the sheer length of the section that slows people down. I noticed more people dropping off the back as we ran through Kendleshire, but without being able to wait for them I kept ploughing on. The clock was ticking.

I hadn't seen Robin or Gareth since the start, but Mark and Jim were both running around the same sort of pace as me, which meant I often caught them up as I reached the checkpoints. Rolling into Hambrook was no different. Looking at my watch we were just a couple of minutes slower than I had accounted for. That wasn't really a problem as there was still a long way to go. But a quick look at the actual time forced me into mental arithmetic mode. Something was wrong but I wasn't sure what. As the rest of the group munched on flapjacks and refilled their bottles, it dawned on me that I hadn't factored in the time we would spend stopped at checkpoints. And that was now adding up. Despite having reached the first two inside my target times, and the third only a couple of minutes over, by the time we left Hambrook we were a whole 14 minutes down. Shit. My rudimentary maths skills had failed me at the worst possible time. The next section to Blaise Estate was a long and hilly one. I would have to move fast to get back on track.

I made the shout and like the pied piper of the Bristol trails, my pack of ten hour time seekers follows me as I moved out towards Bradley Stoke. As we skirted around the wooded edge of the town, we ran through the 32 mile mark. Many of the people still running with me were now well into uncharted territory and naturally all were tiring. I had originally calculated it would take two hours and 35 minutes to cover the 11 miles between checkpoints three and four. As we trudged our way through the fields of Easter Compton and climbed Spaniorum Hill, I had no reason to doubt that would be wrong. That would be a problem. Crossing back over the M5, I took the advantage of being back on Tarmac to pick up the pace a little, but with heavy legs it wasn't an easy task. We had now been running for eight and a half hours and everybody was unsurprisingly flagging. Ten hours was looking doubtful.

We reached the final checkpoint at the ranger's station in Blaise Estate two hours and 27 minutes after leaving Hambrook. That was good news considering I had factored on the section taking a whole eight minutes more. But that was in the old world of timing. The reality was even arriving at the checkpoint with just enough time to refill our bottles and grab a jaffa cake, we would already be leaving 14 minutes later than planned. To make things worse, the final six-and-a-half miles were largely uphill. There was 600 feet of climbing before we reached the finish, which doesn't sound like a lot but when you've run 40 miles it's enough to slow you to a crawl. As I went to leave, I looked around and saw Mark and Jim. "You're not getting this in in ten hours then," shouted Mark. While it didn't look likely, I wasn't ready to accept defeat. That and I like to prove people wrong. "We'll see," I called back smiling.

For the final time I made the call and led the group of now nine runners towards Clifton and the finish at Ashton Court. As we left, I told them of our predicament and gave them a pep talk. "I think we can do this, but it's not going to be easy," I told them. "We will have to run everything but the very steepest climbs and when I say run, I mean at a good pace." While my goal was to get myself in at ten hours, these nine runners had stuck with me for the last 40 miles and had put their faith in my ability to get them around. It was my responsibility to get them back to Ashton Court in good time.

Leaving Blaise, through Sea Mills and on up to Durdham Down we pushed hard. My legs were battered, but every time I picked up the pace the group stuck with me. We had all spent so long together and everyone had spoken to everyone else at some point that we were now running as one. The collective positive attitude grew as we made it further and further into the course. As the miles ticked by and the infamous Clifton Suspension Bridge came into view, I knew it would be a close call. We had made up significant ground over the last few miles and the end was now almost in sight but we weren't there yet.

Entering Ashton Court Estate I passed through the gate into the red deer enclosure and looked at my watch. Nine hours and 54 minutes. I could see the house at the bottom of the hill, but it was still more than half a mile away, down a winding trail and through a car park. I like to think of bounding as a word to describe my action down the hill, but it was probably more like a fast hobbling bounce. As I went through the gate at the bottom of the enclosure and into the car park, my watch ticked over to nine hours and 58 minutes. The rest of the pack was close behind me coming down the hill. With the finish arch in sight I sprinted. Well, in my head I sprinted. The effort it took felt like it should have been a sprint. It was hardly anything that would bother Usain Bolt, but after 45 miles it definitely felt fast. As I crossed the line, I looked down and stopped my watch. Nine hours, 59 minutes and 45 seconds. Job done. While the official time was registered as 31 seconds over the ten hours, it was still close enough to consider it successful. We had run the last six and a half miles in an hour and 10 minutes, a whole 15 minutes faster than I had originally factored for. It wasn't an easy way to finish a race, but the sense of satisfaction at a job well done was incredible. It proved once again that even when tired if you've got the right mental attitude (and somebody telling you it's not possible) that you can push yourself to accomplish amazing things.

Jim and Mark finished together close behind me. A foot injury slowed Mark's progress over the final section from Blaise, but that didn't stop them from running a solid ten hours and 16 minutes - a big personal best for Jim. Gareth's default plan of going out fast worked better for him this time as he had crossed the finish line in an impressive nine hours and 42 minutes. A fantastic performance. Robin finished in 20th place in a time of eight hours and 12 minutes. Of course he did.

18. Revisiting Misery

With the success of my timelord duties carrying me high, I continued to follow my plan. After the race I opted for a couple of lower mileage weeks to recover before heading off on a two-week road trip around Northern California over Easter. As was always the way, I packed my running kit with the full intention of getting some miles in while I was away. I even made sure I booked hotels that had gyms in case I didn't fancy running outside. But the reality of holidays and life on the road meant my trainers stayed firmly at the bottom of the bag for the entire trip. Not a single mile was logged. It wasn't the end of the world though. The schedule already catered for couple of low weeks and in a way it was nice to have a break.

I returned from America light on miles yet heavy on junk food. But I switched back to the training plan and built my mileage back up over the following weeks. We were now approaching the end of April and, looking at the multicolour chart, there was a large black block looming. It was another night run, this time with my nemesis the Cotswold Way.

The Cotswold Way is a 102 mile footpath that runs between Chipping Campden in Gloucestershire and the city of Bath. Over its entire length the path serves up more than 14,000 feet of climbing, with peaks peppered evenly throughout. Living near the Bath end of the trail, Paul and I, together with five others, had used it for what was supposed to have been a 30-mile training run in the lead-up to the Highland Fling. The distance ended up being closer to 33 miles, which doesn't sound like a big difference but it was on that occasion. It was a day that will forever be etched in my memory as horrific. Frankly, it had been the most miserable day of running I have ever experienced. Unusually for me, I left the planning of the route to somebody else. While this was fine, it meant I was oblivious to the true nature of the challenge. Namely, the hills. Who knew the Cotswolds were hilly? Well, me actually. What an idiot. Even looking back with fondness on adventures I've undertaken, there remained no positives I could take from the day. It had been wet, windy, we got lost, ran several miles further than expected, and had been woefully underprepared for such a beast of a trail. The path had chewed us up and spat us back out. It was the run we never spoke of. Until now.

On a run one morning, Paul and I had tried to mentally map out a hard route to bolster our mental endurance. "What's the shittiest run we've ever done? The toughest?" I asked him. He paused while he thought. "Has to be that Cotswold run," he replied. He wasn't wrong and we both knew it. So I said it: "Then we need to do it again. We need to face up to our demons." Paul smiled and nodded. "Agreed. But you know what we need to do? We need to do it at night." As much as I wanted to disagree with him, again he was right. If we were to stand any chance of running 100 miles, through night and day, we needed to be able to deal with a paltry 33 nocturnal miles on the Cotswold Way.

So once again, Paul and I found ourselves standing on a platform at Bristol Temple Meads station on a Friday night waiting for the last train to somewhere. That somewhere being Cam and Dursley in Gloucestershire where we could join the path. From there we would navigate and run back to my house in Bristol. We planned to complete the run in eight hours at the most. It wasn't a random time, but the equivalent pace to running 100 miles in 25 hours. The outcome would be a benchmark.

Arriving at Dursley just before 11pm, we ran through the

sleeping town until we reached the point where the Cotswold Way passed through. Running past The Old Spot Inn, we took a right turn and started our first climb on the trail and into the murky-looking woods. I had the GPS route loaded onto my watch, which was an absolute necessity given neither of us had a clue which way to go. Sure we had run it before, but that was a long time ago and to be honest I was so oblivious at the start, and so miserable by the end, I paid no attention to where we had gone.

As the glow of the streetlights became replaced by the shadow of the trees, we laughed nervously and joked about the journey ahead. It was just the two of us with our head torches against the night. But in our moment of jollity we failed to notice we had already taken a wrong turn and headed off into the forest away from the trail. It was only after we found ourselves in a dead-end that we realised we were lost. Looking down at my watch I could see we were so far from the line we were supposed to be following that it was almost off the screen. I didn't know the scale but it looked a long way. Navigation fail. Getting back on track meant wandering around the darkness seemingly for ages until we eventually found our way back onto what looked like the path. Back on the digital line we moved on to the next place we could get lost. We didn't have to wait long. Over the span of the next half a mile, we misplaced ourselves a further four times. It was going to be a long night.

Back on the correct route, we made our way through the village of North Nibley and took the steep climb up to the William Tyndale monument. We reached the top just after midnight and sat on the bench next to the floodlit tower. Getting something out of my backpack to eat, I looked out over South Gloucestershire below. It was dark and I saw nothing. Running back downhill, we ran through the town of Wotton-under-Edge, past the clearing out of the pubs and the standard shouts of "Run Forrest, run". How we laughed. Original wit is always hilarious. So far the misery of the previous run had yet to materialise and we were having a good night. Even the creepy darkness of the woods held no fear any longer. Could our experience of long runs over the subsequent years have made that much difference to our mental confidence? We were only eight miles in so let's not get carried away. The night was still young.

As with most nights out running, we stopped in the churchyard to refill our bottles, hunting down the tap among the graves by the light of our head torches. Following the national trail signs pointing out of town, we ran along a small brook heading towards the adjacent village of Coombe. As we ran along the narrow path beside the stream, we heard a loud growling. Having eaten back at the monument I knew it wasn't my stomach. That's when we saw a large dog standing in the shallow water. He wasn't paddling, he was facing off with a worried-looking sheep. I'm no dog expert but if I had to guess the breed I'd say it was a big one. A big angry one. It was clear the sheep wasn't a friend of his and would rather not be there. I stopped, trying to decide what to do, but as I turned around to talk to Paul he was already gone. He had vaulted the fence behind me into the next field and an imagined realm of safety. I thought about trying to scare the dog away. But seeing how good a job he was doing at showing his teeth to the sheep, I decided it was probably best to join Paul over the fence and move on as quickly as we could. It was after 1am and there was nobody around to either claim the dog or help us if he wanted to befriend us next. We left nature to take its course and ran on, quickly. Further upstream we came across another sheep in the kind of state that validated our choice to move on.

We carried on climbing out of Wotton up a steep Tarmac lane, then an even steeper set of steps through more woods. Although we were now more carefully following the route on my watch, none of it was looking familiar. Maybe it was the difference between running in day and night, or perhaps I had totally switched off the last time.

But having faith in technology meant following the line regardless. So long as the battery lasted, it would get us home.

As with all long runs we passed the miles with a mixture of inane banter, old stories and brave talk of challenges to come. We kept moving forward, walking whenever we felt like it and running when we could. It was all about ticking off those miles. One after another after another. There was no doubt that the Cotswold Way was a hilly route, but somehow the climbs seemed less brutal than they had done the last time. They still weren't easy but they weren't like climbing Conic Hill before Loch Lomond, or hiking up the mountain to the first checkpoint in Gran Canaria. It was all relative. Everything we had accomplished over the previous three years had helped to transform our perception of this route from a miserable hell into something achievable. We weren't significantly fitter than we had been before but now we had perspective.

Reaching Old Sodbury, we sat on the benches in the garden of The Dog Inn and chowed down on a further combination of savoury and sweet treats. It was just after 4am. We had been up all day, had just run 20 miles and were still 13 miles from home. Tiredness had come and gone in waves but overall we didn't feel too bad. Although our pace had wavered, we were still making good progress. Even after getting lost a couple more times on our way through the Dodington Estate. Reaching the A46 meant breaking from the trail and rather than crossing over into Tormarton, we peeled off to the right and followed the road back towards Bristol. Now on Tarmac with the sun rising to one side of us and back on familiar ground, we picked up the pace and plodded along the long winding road through Westerleigh. From here it was simply a case of getting back onto the cycle path and heading home via the shortest route I could calculate in my sleep-deprived brain.

Six long slow miles later we finally reached my front door. It was just minutes after 7am. We had achieved our goal of running the same miserable 33 mile route in eight hours. Overall we had experienced a completely different run to the time before. Don't get me wrong, it hadn't been easy but it had proved again that with the right frame of mind and realistic expectations we could achieve things we perceived to be difficult. Out of all the runs on the multicolour training plan, it was the one I was most happy to cross off. It was a demon we had faced up to and put down with a vengeance. With just six weeks left on the plan it was a confidence booster and a great place to be. Physically and mentally we were in a strong place. A few more weeks of steady miles and then the tortuous taper to race day began.

19. Don't Be Shit

Reaching the start of June brought the reality of running 100 miles home. With training completed and the race just over a week away I had reduced my mileage to almost nothing. Over the last six months I had run an average of 37 miles a week. It didn't sound like much. For a few weeks I peaked in the low 50s but that hadn't been a common occurrence. I had made a plan and followed it as closely as I could. There had been hills, races, lunchbreaks full of miles and even a few instances where I navigated myself through the night on long trails. But in my head a little voice told me I hadn't done enough. I had averaged similar mileage when training for road marathons in the past. The only difference was that that had been over a shorter time period. But this was four marathons back-to-back - how could the training be the same?

Doubts are entirely natural. The start line of any race is always full of runners thinking they could have done more training. Yet they were there anyway. Getting them through it would be a combination of fitness, confidence in the training they had done and their desire to reach the finish line. Doubts play a part in keeping performance grounded in reality, mostly for the sake of self-preservation. Overall, while it felt like it might not have been enough, it was what I had planned and I couldn't have realistically fitted in much more. Being pragmatic about it, the training I'd done would have to be enough.

I had already proved to myself several times how the mental aspect of a race was just as important as the actual fitness. Being in good physical shape hadn't stopped me from giving up 21 miles into the race across Gran Canaria. Yet I had completed the Green Man Midnight Express on minimal training by being on familiar ground and feeling comfortable about the challenge. The difference in terrain and elevation obviously played a part as well. But with the South Downs Way falling somewhere between the two, my mental approach to this race would be key to its success. That was clear.

One of the issues Paul and I had suffered during Transgrancanaria had been slow progress. This convinced us that we were going to be timed out at a checkpoint and it played a part in our mental downfall. Thinking we wouldn't make the cut-offs, we quit. But according to the wisdom of experienced ultrarunner James Adams, thinking you are going to miss the cut-offs is not a reason for dropping out, *missing* the cut-offs is a reason for dropping out. Don't worry about something until it happens is the key, because it might not happen. It sounded like the kind of simple idea for overcoming negative thinking I had learnt from cognitive behavioural therapy. Clearly it was one I hadn't remembered. Over the previous months I had collated as much information as I could, and spoken to everyone I knew who had already run the distance to pick their brains for titbits of experience. It had all been helpful stuff and I had tucked it away for retrieval when I really needed it.

In the final week before the race I went out with Bear for a slow lunchtime jog and we chatted about his experience of the South Downs Way. You see, the previous year it hadn't only been Paul who I had persuaded to enter, but Bear as well. But whereas Paul and I had pulled out before even getting close to the start line, Bear saw it through and finished in a solid 27 hours. If anybody knew what I was about to go through, Bear did.

We talked about all aspects of the race, but it was the low points in particular I needed to understand. For Bear, the last 40 miles had been miserable and the final 30 torture. Having made it to halfway feeling strong, he progressively slowed down as he became more and more tired. This was where his mental endurance kicked in. He explained how at 75 miles he wanted nothing more than to stop. He was tired, sore and really not enjoying it. Keeping going wasn't something he held any interest in. But that sentiment was offset by the desire to finish. "I told myself I wanted to run 100 miles, and stopping now meant I would have to come back and go through all that misery again only to be at the same point," he explained, "it was just easier to keep going."

It was a twisted logic but it revealed perfectly the mental torment of such a challenge. By three-quarters of the way through, you've already covered the bulk of the distance. Why throw all that away? There will always be times when dropping out of a race is the sensible option, especially if you're likely to end up injured by continuing. But if the only thing being damaged is your pride then it becomes less clear cut. You knew it was going to be tough when you signed up. Wasn't that the point? The single best piece of advice Bear gave me, however, was the simplest: "You just have to really want it. More than anything else, you have to want it. If you don't, you won't make it." It made sense. To talk yourself out of the darkest of times, reaching the end has to be your overriding thought. As we made our way back to the office, Bear offered me the ultimate lifeline. He told me that if I was thinking of quitting, at any time of the day or night, then to call him. Pick up the phone and explain to him why I was going to drop out and he would remind me why I was doing it. You can't ask for better support than that.

With the race setting off from Winchester at 6am on Saturday morning, Paul and I drove down the evening before. That meant we could collect our numbers, grab a bite to eat and hopefully get a reasonable amount of sleep before the start. As we eased our way along the A303 in rush hour traffic, we talked about our plan for the race. Quietly in the background, on BBC Radio 2, Simon Mayo was talking to callers on his drivetime show. I heard the trigger phrase

'South Downs Way' come out of the car speakers and I turned up the volume. The person on the end of the phone had just explained to Simon how her husband was running a 100 mile race this weekend from Winchester to Eastbourne. Simon was incredulous: "Wow! He's running 100 miles? How? Why?" I looked at Paul and we both laughed. This was a common response and one we had come to expect. Between ourselves and our running friends, discussions would normally continue past the exclamation of distance, as if running 100 miles was a perfectly normal thing to do. But for people not familiar with ultrarunning, the big numbers were often unsurprisingly a conversation stopper. As the talking on the radio stopped, *Keep On Running* by the Spencer Davis Group started. A symbolic but obvious choice. I turned the radio back down again.

We drove directly to Chilcomb Sports Ground where the mandatory kit check and registration was taking place. Like most ultra events there was a list of minimum required kit you had to carry and that kit needed to be checked before your race number would be handed over. From a road running perspective that might seem a tad overbearing, but you have to consider how long the runners would be out on the course. An average 100 mile race (if such a thing exists) would have a cut-off of around 30 hours. That's a day and a quarter out on a trail, potentially in poor weather and often with nowhere to hide. Mandatory kit could be a lifesaver.

Kit check passed and numbers collected, we stood around surveying where our challenge would begin the following morning and watching the other runners picking up their numbers. Trying to take it all in, my head was whizzing with excitement. Where was the start? Which way would we go? Shit, this is my race number! This is real! "Alright Ira? How are you?" I looked around and saw a vaguely familiar face, but not one I could instantly place. "It's Mark. We met at the Green Man." Still nothing. Without being able to put a name to a face, despite having just been given a name, I defaulted to

142

my standard: "Alright mate, how you doing?" As we talked, I played the biding my time game, trying to work out who I was talking to and where the common ground lay. Paul walked over and joined us. I introduced the two of them. "This is Paul, Paul this is Jon," I said confidently. "Actually it's Mark," he countered. Busted! I glossed over it and we continued to chat. After another couple of minutes the penny dropped. It was Mark Thornberry. Somebody I had met in the past and talked to often on Twitter. Sometimes I worry about the state of my memory. Perhaps my next book should be called *Still Can't Remember.*

We drove the short distance from the sports ground to our hotel, with Mark and his friend Ilsuk squeezed into the back of my car. Luckily for their legs it was a short journey. After checking in we took our bags up to our room and I took a photo of my race number and posted it to Twitter together with a link to the live online tracking. On the bottom of the number I had already written my mantra for the following day in permanent marker: '#DontBeShit'. A simple yet effective hashtag to remind me of what I needed to do. Or rather *not* do. My phone instantly went into meltdown with messages of luck and support rolling back in. It was uplifting to know so many people out there were rooting for me; both friends and strangers. It was like a remote support network feeding me positive vibes over the ether. I wasn't quite sure of the correct social media etiquette on how to deal with so many replies. Ignoring them was clearly rude but replying to them all personally would take forever. Even more so if I actually typed a personal note back to each one. I opted for a hybrid approach with randomly selected replies of "cheers dude!" and "thanks mate".

After a short walk around the local Tesco for some breakfast items and last minute supplies, we made our way back to the hotel and down to the restaurant for an early dinner. Steak and chips for two, please. The dining room was full of faces I recognised. Runners

I knew who were also taking on the South Downs Way. I don't know what the collective noun for crazy fools is but that room seemed to be housing it. They were all early diners, many nursing a solitary beer in a bid to relax before an early start followed by a very long run.

Mark and Ilsuk were sitting at the table next to us and we talked about our plans for the run. Unlike Paul and me, both of them had already run the distance before so knew what to expect. We were just going to have to take it all as it came. It would all be one big learning curve. No matter how many times you read somebody's account, or someone explains to you how you might feel at various stages of the race, it would never be the same as first-hand experience. There may be several hundred people on the start line come the morning, but as with running any distance, getting to the finish would ultimately be a very personal battle.

Returning to our room, Paul and I checked our kit for the final time. Shoehorned into my racing vest were a few essentials such as tissues, foil blanket and a first aid kit as well as a stock of gels, a hearty supply of electrolyte replacement capsules, a Ginsters steak slice and some honey and salt roasted peanuts. I also squeezed a few bags of sweets in there for good measure. It was an eclectic mix of ingredients for a day out. Alongside the various items of food supplied at the checkpoints, I was hoping it would be enough to get me through. As I lay on the bed, a frightening realisation dawned over me. I had forgotten something. I turned to Paul: "Shit! I haven't asked what colour the finisher shirt was. I hope it isn't orange." It was too late now if it was.

With nothing more to do except the running, we talked about what we expected from the day. Our goal was simply to finish. Rather than put any time pressure on ourselves, reaching Eastbourne inside the 30-hour cut-off was the only thing that mattered. If I crossed the finish line even just one second under the time limit, I would be ecstatic. It was about as low pressure as you could make running 100 miles.

Having read the info pack on the race website as well as signing a disclaimer when collecting our numbers, our conversation turned to the serious nature of looking after ourselves. This wasn't a city road race, or a four or five hour trail marathon where you could afford to be a little reckless, this was a serious undertaking. In the medical section of the information a list highlighted ten conditions to be aware of. These were preceded by the following statement: "Some of the main risks, but certainly not all of them, are listed here. These should be understood and remembered by all runners, before and during the event. Please note that death can result from several of the risk conditions discussed below." Death. That's dying from running. It didn't get more serious than that. Sweet dreams.

STILL NOT BIONIC

20. All Day and All of the Night

As the alarm went off at 4am, I wondered if I'd had any sleep at all. It didn't feel like it. Between the nerves and the heating, it had felt more restless than restful. I made coffee and soaked a few Weetabix in a bowl. I figured eating what I could now would be a good idea. It was still two hours until the start, but with the combination of pre-race bathroom preparations, the commute to the start and ensuring we were there in plenty of time, it wasn't an overly loose schedule.

Arriving at the sports ground for the start there were considerably more people than there had been on Friday evening. I parked my car at the far end of the field out of the way, ready for collection on Sunday afternoon, and walked down towards the start. All Centurion races sell out and quickly. It's a reflection on the quality of the events they put on. They hold four 100 mile races every year and each of them caters for around 300 runners. Walking around the crowd my head was buzzing. This was it. Not just the sharp point of the last six months of training, or even the chance to put right pulling out the year before, but it was an opportunity to prove to myself that I could take the next step up in ultra distance running. I had proved to myself time and again that I could grind out flattish 40 and 50 mile races. Physically fit or not, mentally I had the endurance to pull it off. But throw in any serious amount of climbing and extend the distance well outside of my comfort zone and my head gave up. This was my chance to change that. Mentally I was ready. I wanted it. I felt as if I was at the narrow end of a funnel and everything that had gone before, right back to the dark clouds of my mental breakdown and turning into the path of that truck, had fed into this moment. The race failures, the arguments with my wife, learning how to deal with my own head when it turned against me… it had all merged and condensed down to this point in time. This event. I had never been so determined of anything in my life. Short of a serious injury that rendered me immobile, I was absolutely going to finish this race.

Walking around before the start, Paul and I bumped into Robin. I knew he was running but with him unable to get a hotel in town we hadn't seen him the night before. This was also his first 100 mile race. Naturally he was nervous as well, but rather than our simple goal of survival he was planning on trying to run under 24 hours. Running a Centurion event in less than one day meant you received a larger belt buckle than the standard finisher one. If anyone could do it I was sure Robin could. Wishing him luck we made our own way to the middle of the starting pack. That would be the last we saw of him. As with all other ultra events Paul and I had run, we decided to start together and keep it that way for as long as possible. If at any point one of us felt stronger, then we agreed they should push on. One-hundred miles is a long way to run and you need to run your own race at your own speed. We had always been well-matched in terms of ability and until now staying together had worked well, but this was different. If surviving the distance meant doing it on our own, then that is how it needed to be.

Standing on the start line just before 6am, the race director James Elson gave us a race briefing. There was a lot of information to take in and I wasn't sure all of it had stuck. But the way he conducted the briefing was rousing. When asked to raise your hand if this was your first 100 mile race almost half of the field did so. To counter the novices, the next show of hands was for those who had already completed all four Centurion races in a single year and had gained the prestigious Grand Slam. There were plenty of those as well. We were in good company.

With such a long route to cover and 14 checkpoints to staff, we were told there were going to be around 180 volunteers looking after us for the duration. It was an incredible amount of people giving up their time to look after the 259 runners who had made it as far as the start line. Many of the volunteers were runners, with plenty also having already completed Centurion events. As much as anybody possibly could, they would have a good insight into the challenges we all faced ahead and the demons we would need to overcome to cover the distance.

The air horn sounded right on time and we were off. Paul and I looked at each other and smiled nervously. This was it. We ran a loop around the edge of the field taking us back down to a corner close to where we had started, before dropping through a gap in the hedge and down onto the South Downs Way itself. All we had to do now was follow the path all the way to Eastbourne. In navigation terms it sounded easy. The South Downs Way, much like the Cotswold Way, is a national trail and as such is well signposted. Alongside the trail signs, Centurion had also decorated the route with red and white reflective tape tied to posts, trees and fences throughout. As with following the trail in Gran Canaria, if you hadn't seen a sign or any tape for a while then you were probably going in the wrong direction. As a backup I had loaded the route onto my GPS watch, which I could use to help navigate should I need to. I wasn't planning on using it unless I had to though, as turning on the navigation used more power and would quickly drain the battery. I had an external battery in my vest and this time I even made sure I'd also packed the cables so I could charge on the go if I needed to. According to the manufacturer, with the navigation off the battery should last at least 24 hours and possibly all the way to Eastbourne if I was lucky.

Safely tucked inside one of my pockets was a small laminated timecard I had produced. It was my bible for the race. On it was a list of all of the checkpoints together with what an estimated 24 hour finish time would be at each location. The second column showed me the cut-off time for the checkpoint and a third showed the same information but as an elapsed time, to save having to calculate anything while on the move. I knew I wouldn't finish in under 24 hours, so the first column was really a warning to stop me from going too fast. If I could stay somewhere between the 24 hour and the cut-off column then I knew I'd be safely on-track.

The start of any race is the point where you always need to be mindful of pace. With a whole pack of runners setting off together, those at the front will naturally pull everyone else along. With the first checkpoint being almost ten miles in, it was a long way to go before being able to judge if we were going too quickly. The problem was it wouldn't feel like we were running fast, as even a 24 hour finish would average just over a 14 minute mile if you could pace it evenly (which you couldn't). It was easy to see how you could get carried away at the start.

The weather was still cool but with a forecast for it to warm up later. That was definitely something to be wary of, making sure we drank plenty and often as well as keeping on top of our electrolyte capsules, which would help keep levels safe. We had decided on a plan of one capsule per hour, every hour. That was important to remember because if electrolyte levels dropped too low then we would run the risk of cramps, feeling nauseous and even potentially suffering hyponatremia, which could be fatal.

Exercise-associated hyponatremia is defined by Wikipedia as "a fluid-electrolyte disorder caused by a decrease in sodium levels during or up to 24 hours after prolonged physical activity. This disorder can develop when marathon runners or endurance event athletes drink more fluid, usually water or sports drinks, than their kidneys can excrete. This excess water can severely dilute the level of sodium in the blood needed for organs, especially the brain, to function properly." There was so much to consider and remember.

As it was still very early in the race our mood was jovial and we felt fresh. While the day heated up and we jogged our way through the first few miles, we smiled and joked across farms, fields and the occasional section of Tarmac. We were having fun. The first nine-mile section to the Beacon Hill checkpoint was a little up and down, but nothing with any serious amount of climbing. Most of the big hills were in the second half of the race. That was something to look forward to.

With the temperature increasing and being mindful of hydration, we decided to make sure we stopped to take a wee at least every hour, checking the colour of our urine. Ideally it should be a light straw colour. If it looked more like cider and blackcurrant you'd know you were in trouble. Too dark and we would make sure to drink more but still not excessively so.

As we reached the first checkpoint we showed our numbers and moved to the food table. A quick glance at my crib sheet told me we had already gone out too quickly. With my estimate of a 24 hour runner passing through at 8:20am, I was surprised to see it was still only 7:54am. I marked it down to early nerves and being dragged along with the pack. Note to self: slow down.

Looking at the buffet on offer I picked up a handful of things to munch on. Another couple of great tips I had been given before the race had been: one - just eat enough food to get you to the next checkpoint, and two - always carry a small plastic bag with you. Rather than hang around at a checkpoint treating it like a picnic, load up your plastic bag with all the treats you fancy and move straight on. Walk out of the checkpoint while eating from your party bag. That way you don't waste any time. It made perfect sense. Given most of the checkpoints (although not this one) were at the bottom of hills, we would naturally be walking out of them anyway. Bags loaded, we moved on towards Queen Elizabeth Country Park (QECP) and the next checkpoint. At just over the 22 mile point it was almost a half-marathon away. Under normal circumstances that would be a long way, but in the grand scheme of the day if wasn't significant.

The second section of the course was considerably hillier than the first with more than 1,000 feet of climbing. Unsurprisingly this slowed our pace as we walked the hills, which given our fast pace earlier wasn't a bad thing. Passing through more fields we found ourselves on the hard chalk trail so characteristic of the South Downs. It was solid underfoot and rutted, but easy enough to run on. After a couple of long climbs we slowly made our way to the top of Butser Hill. On reaching the summit we had peaked at the highest point of the entire path. The view from the top was stunning and brought an involuntary smile to my face. This was what running was about, this was what adventure was about. Incredible views, miles laid out before us and good friends for company.

With the A3 cutting through the valley below, a steady string of runners bounded their way down the hill towards the next checkpoint. At around 10:40am Paul and I reached the QECP aid station and once again loaded up our plastic bags for the hike up through the woods on the other side. I pulled out my timecard to check how our pace was holding up. We were still going too fast. My 24 estimate would pass through at 11:20am. We had picked up even more time over the last section. It hadn't seemed like we had been going that quickly, especially considering the hills we walked. I began to question where I got the times from and if my number skills had let me down again. Perhaps the whole timecard was flawed. That wouldn't be good. You could always look at it as time in the bank, knowing you will probably slow down later anyway. But the concern was how much that faster pace would affect your legs later on. The day was really starting to warm up now with the sun higher in the sky. I took the precaution of wearing a white cap to protect my balding head, which I made sure to dowse with water regularly to keep me cool. Out on most of the trail there was nowhere to hide from the sun and it would be easy to be affected by it if we weren't careful. So far we had managed to keep on top of it, but it was still early and the day was only going to get hotter.

Hiking up through the forest that made up the bulk of the country park, I snacked on various things from my doggy bag. With the usual cakes and sweets hard to swallow on the move, I found the fresh fruit on offer amazing. Satsuma segments, strawberries, watermelon and especially the pineapple. Wow, the pineapple! It was sweet and refreshing.

From here on the checkpoints were much closer together. The next one on the list was Harting Downs at 27 miles. As we hit the chalk trail and started running again, the thought struck me that the numbers seemed paradoxical. In my head I had the conflicting thoughts that I had now already run a marathon and that was a long way. Yet at the same time I was still only a quarter of the way through the race. It was hard to reconcile the two strands. Had I run a long way or not? For the sake of the bigger picture I had to convince myself that I hadn't run very far. If I allowed myself to accept I had, then my brain would melt trying to contemplate what still lay ahead. Mentally I was feeling fine, physically surprisingly so, too.

The next five miles passed by relatively quickly and, still running together, Paul and I arrived at Harting Downs. My watch told me we were still running a fast time, having arrived 30 minutes under my 24 hour estimate. Clearly slowing down wasn't working too well. As we loaded up our doggy bags I wondered if we hadn't misjudged our abilities and we were doing ourselves a disservice by not consciously trying to hang on to the faster pace for as long as we could. It was a positive thought but a dangerous one. After spending so long trying to battle the negative thoughts in my head, trying to eject a positive one was an odd concept. But if I listened to my errant delusional optimism then I could end up never making it to Eastbourne. I told myself to not get suckered in and stick to the plan. The time was immaterial and the end was still a very long way off.

Unfortunately, the next eight-mile section to Cocking started to prove my rational thought right. The sun was high now and it was becoming hot. Passing through the 30-mile point my stomach had started to become unsettled and it was apparent Paul had started to pull away from me. I wasn't sure if he was speeding up or if I was slowing down. But the end result was the same. I didn't try to fight it or ask him to slow down, as it was better for him to push on if he could. I just kept my head down and plugged on. With the hills coming frequently now, the going was starting to get tougher. It was hot, I was starting to tire and my stomach wasn't enjoying itself. All this and I still had 70 miles to go. Just get to the next checkpoint I kept telling myself. Just get to the checkpoint.

Dropping down the long gravelly chalk trail to the Cocking checkpoint, I could see Paul ahead of me. He knew I wasn't far behind so was dawdling his way down the hill. As we crossed the main road and entered the field where the gazebo was erected, I took off my vest and sat down on the grass. I was desperate for a drink, having run out of water a couple of miles earlier and glugged down a full bottle. I wanted to eat something, too, but wasn't sure if my stomach would take it. Talking to the marshals I heard people were dropping out through heat exhaustion. Affected by the sun and unable to keep anything down, their races were already over. It was a gutting thought. I put a few snacks in my bag, tucked it into my vest and paid a visit to the Portaloo.

Sitting in a chemical toilet in the middle of field after you've run 35 miles is a sobering prospect. As I sat in the smelly enclosed space, I played out various scenarios in my head. Was I sick enough to drop out? Was this going to get any better or easier? Experience told me it was common to feel nauseous as you start to get tired, but with 65 miles still to go it was a long way to run while feeling queasy. The thought entered my head that if I was going to drop I would need to call Bear and explain myself. But explain what exactly? That I was a bit tired and had a sore tummy? I delved into my mental toolkit and addressed my negative issues one by one. I wasn't sick, I wasn't injured and I wasn't being timed out. This show was moving on. As I left the checkpoint, Paul was a short distance ahead of me. I had been sat around for about 15 minutes, most of which he had patiently waited for me. "Catch me up," he shouted back to me as he pushed on. I told him I would but I wasn't entirely convinced.

It was long slow climb coming out of Cocking and with Paul's head start I knew I wasn't likely to catch him. In truth I didn't want to. As much as the company was always great, he was clearly in a better state than me and I didn't want to hold him up. I also didn't want to be dragged along. It was six miles to Bignor Hill and the next checkpoint, a distance that included two very steep uphill sections. In the strong heat of the afternoon I kept my head down and ploughed on at a steady pace. I needed to get to 50 miles. It was a distance I'd only covered once before, and going past that I would be in unknown territory. But it was also halfway and the point at which I could starting counting down and not up. It would be a small psychological win.

Letting Paul pull away felt like a good move. I naturally eased my pace and was now in control of my own destiny. Despite the earlier wobble, my stomach had started to feel a little better and my confidence was back on the rise. I passed through Bignor Hill without stopping for too long and pushed on for the next nine mile slog to the halfway point. My pace was slower now but it was also driven. There weren't too many people still around me at this point, which didn't particularly bother me. I am always comfortable with my own company and was enjoying taking in the scenery as I plodded along the chalk ridge. As the miles increased and the illusory oasis of the halfway mark edged onto the horizon, my mood began to improve. Much like the paradox of the marathon marker earlier in the day, it was almost wrong to celebrate having just as much left to run as I had already covered, but the ability to flip between less miles to the finish than back to the start made selling myself the idea of keeping going much easier.

Cruelly the halfway mark sat atop a 600 feet climb and wasn't even signposted as such. Despite everything that had already gone on, I passed through 50 miles in a personal best time for the distance. Having only run it once before I wasn't sure if it really counted but I took it as a positive anyway. I took out my phone and posted a celebratory Tweet: "Through 50 in 12 hours. Over halfway. Taking this mother to a retirement home in Eastbourne. Smoke me a kipper, I'll be back for breakfast." I thought it was funny and was pleased with myself for coming up with something so witty. I'd had plenty of time to think of it.

Passing quickly through the checkpoint at Kithurst Hill, I pushed onwards towards the next one at Washington and the 54 mile mark. Whereas every checkpoint so far had hosted a fantastic buffet of snacks, the next one had all that plus hot meals. It was also the location of the first of two drop bags we could access on the course. I had put in a bag for here and another for Clayton Windmills.

As I ran down the road towards the village hall where the checkpoint was based, I passed Paul who was just leaving. "Catch me up, I'm going to walk for a bit," he shouted over. It was a nice idea but so was sitting down and having some hot food. I wandered into the hall and was immediately swarmed by a gang of volunteers asking me what they could get for me. Before I knew it my drop bag was in my hands. Hot food? Refill my bottles? It was like having a team of personal servants at your beck and call. They were absolutely incredible and even writing this now makes my eyes leak a little at how much of a difference they made to the journey. Thank you all so much.

In my drop bag I had a change of socks and shirt, as well as a stick of Bodyglide to re-lube myself to prevent chaffing. I popped to the bathroom, re-applied the lubricant on and around my thighs before sitting in a chair and being served a glorious dish of pasta bolognaise. It was 7:11pm when I had arrived and I had now been running for more than 13 hours. A plate of hot food and a change of clothes was like winning the lottery. As I took off my old socks, I noticed a large blister on the side of my right big toe. I contemplated cutting it open and putting a dressing on it, but as it wasn't giving me any trouble I decided the best option was probably to just leave it well alone. Due to the lack of anything more suitable, I wrapped it in a length of masking tape. I wasn't sure if that would protect it, but I figured it couldn't make it any worse. Dressed in fresh clothes and with newly oiled thighs, I left Washington like a new man heading out for a night on the town.

With more distance behind me than still left to cover I slowly climbed the steep 650 feet to the top of the next hill. Paul hadn't reckoned on two things when he suggested I catch him up. Firstly the fact that I would sit at the checkpoint for half an hour, and secondly that with a climb of this magnitude I would be walking it as well. I didn't see him again.

With nobody around me, I plugged myself into my iPod and fired up my playlist of kick-ass songs to keep me moving. I'm not usually a fan of running to music, I find it annoying, but the idea was to try and break the run up a bit and provide some mental distraction. It worked. Running slowly down the chalk path I smiled and laughed to myself as I belted out *Highway To Hell* by AC/DC to the sheep in the adjacent field. Judging by their reactions, I don't think they were rock fans.

As seemed to be the way with the South Downs, after I had reached the top of the hill, the next seven miles was spent running straight back down again. Trying to run nearly 800 feet down to sea level at this point in the race was a quad-smasher. By the time I reached the bottom, even shuffling was painful. Luckily the next checkpoint was at the lowest point on the path. As I entered and gave them my number they looked me up on the list to check me off. The marshal with the clipboard in hand looked at me and laughed. "I've got a copy of your book at home," she said, "I love it. Can I get a picture with you?" So at 9:30pm and after running 61 miles I posed for a selfie with a total stranger. Not just any total stranger but one who was giving up their day to help me in my quest to run 100 miles. Obliging her request was the very least I could do. As I smiled and posed, a man peeled a satsuma and broke it into individual segments for me. Another tucked freshly filled water bottles into my vest. It was one of the most surreal moments of my life. It made me smile and gave me a boost like nothing else could. I was back in the realm of firmly wanting this more than anything else.

Leaving the checkpoint with almost 40 miles still to run, it had started to get dark. Night was falling and I had put my head torch on ready. The darkness would be thrown across an unfamiliar and remote countryside that I would face alone, with nothing more than a bulb strapped to my head. I wasn't sure I knew who I was any more. Two years earlier, the idea of running on a deserted trail through the night by myself would've scared the shit out me, but I had done it so many times now that it was really no different to doing it during the day. There was just less of a view. The only difference between then and now was experience and that was all in my head.

The next climb was the longest and possibly close to the steepest of all the hills on the path. With 60 miles already in my legs, a continuous two-and-a-half mile climb to the top would take me another hour. As I passed a remote YHA hostel near the top I thought about how lovely it would be to go in and lie down. Even in a dormitory with everyone else snoring. I let the fantasy go and carried on slowly. From the top of the hill I could make out a few head torches moving though the valley ahead of me but nobody was close. I wondered for a moment whether one of them was Paul and how far ahead he still was. But it was impossible to tell.

With 35 miles still to go and visibility reduced to only the path directly in front of me, I took the decision to mostly hike my way through the night. Not a Sunday afternoon ramble but a power walk. A purposeful trek. My logic was two-fold. Firstly, by moving slower I would be less likely to miss signs or tape in the darkness and hence not get lost, and secondly it meant tripping over rocks, roots and falling down a hole was also more unlikely. Plus it broke up the journey slightly with a change of pace. Making it to daybreak in one piece was the goal. With my iPod still playing, Farley Jackmaster Funk explained to me how *Love Can't Turn Around*. The miles were slowly ticking by and soon I found my way past Devil's Dyke and into the next checkpoint at Saddlescombe Farm. The distance was 66.6 miles. I could make some cheap joke about having descended into Hell but to be honest the volunteers were more akin to angels than demons. With fairy lights strung across the barn, a table full of sweet and savoury treats and a gang of smiling faces, I took up residence in a camping chair with a cup of coffee in one hand and a cup of soup in the other.

The time was just before 11:20pm. I had now been running for 17 hours and 20 minutes and had covered two-thirds of the course. With an optimistic slant that was a huge distance behind me, but with a pessimistic one I still had half of that to go again. I took out my timecard and tried to focus on where I was. The 24 hour pace that I had managed to keep under for the first 40 miles had long since slid away. I was now an hour and a half behind it. That was fine though, as I was still more than two and a half hours ahead of the cut-off. It did highlight, however, my slowing pace. Keeping ahead of the cut-off times was key in my mind now. I figured my plan to mostly walk until dawn was still valid so long as I kept moving quickly. 'Quickly' being a relative term here.

Leaving the comfort of a chair and hot soup behind my mood was mixed. I was still doing well, but the jubilation I experienced back at Washington had long since worn away. I was tired, alone and quite frankly a little bored of keeping going. I told myself to get a grip, skipped my iPod to Michael McDonald singing *Sweet Freedom* and continued my climb on towards Clayton Windmills and the next checkpoint. "We'll be dancin' in the moonlight, Smilin' with the risin' sun, Livin' like we've never done, Goin' all the way." Wise words, Mike.

It was only a short matter of three miles to the next checkpoint but with several more hills to contend with and legs that were starting to feel like lumps of wood my progress was incredibly slow. My phone pinged with an incoming text message. It was my wife who was lying awake in bed wondering how I was getting on. Occasional notes of support out of the blue were a welcome boost after so long on my own. It reminded me that even in the middle of the dark countryside, miles from anywhere, I was never on my own.

As I made my way up past Pyecombe Golf Club I looked around desperately for a windmill. That would mean I could stop again and hopefully get something else hot to drink. It was really starting to get chilly and keeping warm through the night was going to be important.

Distance-wise, all I had to go by was my GPS watch. While it can prove invaluable for navigation, you have to remember the distance recorded is likely not to be exact. As I reached the top of the climb, according to my watch I was already more than half a mile past the checkpoint yet I hadn't seen anything. No people, no signs, no tape and definitely no windmills. When you're tired and unable to think straight it's easy to assume you've gone the wrong way and then start making rash decisions like turning around. With nothing in clear sight and nobody around me, I stopped in the lane and didn't know what to do. My mind had lost the power of rational thought. After what seemed like forever, but in reality was probably only a minute or two, I shuffled on a little further looking for some kind of sign. Out of the darkness, like the tiniest gathering of fireflies, I saw a string of lights. As I moved closer I realised they were in fact more fairy lights. Like the runway lights at an airport they were there to safely guide us to the checkpoint. They were a beautiful sight.

I walked into the aid station and slumped into another camping chair. There were other runners in there, all in various states of exhaustion. It was the first time I'd seen anybody since I'd left Saddlescombe Farm, which seemed like forever. With a fresh cup of sugary coffee in hand I consulted my timecard. It was 12:34am. Still two hours and 20 minutes inside the cut-off. There was still plenty of time but it was also slipping away dangerously quickly. The combination of the darkness, having been on the move for 18-and-a-half hours and increasingly sore legs was really beginning to take its toll. I still had 30 miles before I reached Eastbourne and in them some of the biggest and longest climbs of the entire course. As I sat stiffening up in the chair, my head began to slowly fill with negative thoughts on making it that far. What was I thinking? Another 30 miles? What a twat. Who cares anyway? Just stop now. It was time to leave the checkpoint before those negative thoughts took hold.

I followed the chain of fairy lights out of the car park and back to the path. Back on my own, I continued up the hill towards Ditchling Beacon - billed by the National Trust as the top of the world. I certainly wasn't going to argue with that. It was a tough climb. On a clear day the views from the summit must've been incredible, but at 1:30am there was only blackness. I looked down at my watch. I was passing through the 72 mile point, and told myself I only had *about* a marathon left to go. That framed the remaining distance into something familiar. I'd finished lots of marathon distance runs. In our training for Transgrancanaria, Paul and I had run seven marathons in nine weeks. It was a distance I was comfortable with. That said, I'd never run one after having already done three of them back-to-back the same day.

With still more than three hours until sunrise, I decided the key thing to focus on was making it through the night. If I could keep moving at a steady pace and didn't lose much more time, hopefully by dawn the combination of daylight and being that bit closer to the finish would lift my spirits. It was time for more musical distraction. I pushed the play button on my iPod and attempted to pick up the pace while simultaneously remembering the lyrics to *Enter Sandman* by Metallica.

Rocking myself along the dark trail, I pushed on steadily, eventually catching up with another runner. She looked like she was struggling and I asked if she was alright. It was a stupid question really, she clearly wasn't but it was a conversation starter. Her name was Sigrid and she was having a problem keeping any food or water down. She had been unable to stomach anything for hours and subsequently had become physically drained. From somewhere in the depths of my brain I recognised it could be a symptom of heat exhaustion. If she was unable to eat or drink anything, keeping moving was going to get increasingly tougher. It was dark, we were alone on the trail and we were at least four miles until the next checkpoint. It was clear I couldn't leave her out there alone. It didn't even merit a second thought. I may have been slowing down and the cut-offs getting tighter, but at the very least I had to make sure she got to the next aid station. As we marched along, we talked about the previous 19 hours and our other experiences of running ultra events. It turned out this wasn't Sigrid's first ultra, nor even her first 100 miler. A German national living in the Netherlands, she was a seasoned ultrarunner who had run races all over the world. The incredible thing was that not only had she also run the Green Man Ultra, but she had also been one of the many runners who had become a DNF statistic at Transgrancanaria the previous year. Even though we had very different backgrounds and came from different parts of the world, we had plenty of common ground to talk about. And talking passed the time.

Despite moving slowly, and almost getting lost and needing to finally turn on the navigation on my watch, the time passed quickly. Before we knew it we were stumbling into Housedean Farm and the next aid station at 76 miles. It was just after 3am and we were now less than two hours inside the cut-off. I knew time was slipping away and it would get tighter but I needed to rest for a while, so I once again slumped into a camping chair. Sigrid hunted around the table of food for things she might be able to keep down. Plain crisps seemed to be bland enough to not make her vomit, so slowly and steadily she ate as many as she could. Our initial conversation had revolved around her reaching the checkpoint safely. I'm not sure either of us thought that she would continue past that point. But after a rest, some ready salted and a touch of milk she was feeling well enough to push on cautiously. Knowing she was feeling more comfortable and confident about carrying on, I decided to leave by myself and pushed on in an attempt to try and make up some lost time.

It had been an hour and a half since I convinced myself I only had *about* a marathon left to go, and yet here I was with *about* a marathon still left to go. It was like Groundhog Day. With 21 hours behind me it was time to try and start moving again at a decent pace. There were four very sizable climbs before Eastbourne and I needed to make every minute count. The next section of eight miles would see me drop under the 20 miles remaining mark, and experience my second dawn since getting up in Winchester. The start seemed like such a long time ago now. It was almost like another lifetime. I decided to push all memory of it to the back of my mind and think of it as a different run on a different day. This was now just any other long slow run. Albeit one where I was pretty tired. There were now only three more checkpoints between me and the finish. From a starting list of 14 that only highlighted further how little I had left to go.

The next checkpoint to get to was Southease. This was located at mile 84, and in my head was on the home straight. Just keep moving until you get there, is all I kept telling myself. But exhaustion was really starting to kick in. As the sun began to rise I caught myself suddenly jolting awake, like snoozing on the sofa in front of the television and catching your head as it falls. To wake with a start meant I must have been asleep. I didn't know for how long but I was still running. My body was on automatic. Stopping to rub my eyes in a desperate attempt to stop myself from dozing off again, I looked up and saw a double decker bus on the trail in front of me. A big red London double decker bus with Eastbourne as the destination. I rubbed my eyes again to make sure I wasn't seeing things, but when I opened them it was clear I had been. It was gone. The bus had vanished but had been replaced with a full skyline of high-rise buildings. I was in the middle of the Sussex countryside and yet in front of me was a full sized city complete with skyscrapers, bus stops and strangely even wind turbines. I rubbed my eyes again and everything disappeared. I was hallucinating through sleep deprivation. My mind had thought it would be funny to play tricks on me. It couldn't play me a trick showing me something positive like I'd already finished, though. As I stood there for a moment contemplating reality, I heard a metal gate slamming some distance behind me. I turned around and saw another runner, about 300 metres away, entering a field I wasn't in. Not only had I been seeing things, but I had also veered off the path and was on the road to nowhere. It had been a close call.

Getting back on the right track and leaving my imaginary city behind, I ran down the long hill into Southease and the checkpoint near the railway station. Despite my legs screaming, the descent made a steady pace possible and after a long stretch of walking before Housedean Farm it was nice to feel like I was properly moving again. At the railway station I was directed over the bridge between platforms by two very cheery volunteers and pointed towards the aid station a little further up the road. It was 5:25am and a warm cup of sugary tea was my breakfast for the day. I wasn't in the mood for eating anything else. In my head the only thing I wanted now was to get to the end. It was 16 miles to Eastbourne and, regardless of how I felt physically, mentally I was confident. It was now all about how long those last 16 miles were going to take. I was still one-hour and 45 minutes inside the cut-off time and every step I took towards the finish made that less of a concern. Cruelly, two of the longest and steepest climbs on the route were now standing between me and my buckle. But that was mere circumstance. I'd got this far and a couple of hills weren't going to stop me now.

Jogging out of the checkpoint towards Alfriston I received a text message from my sister, who after tracking me until the early hours had now woken up, checked the website again and saw I was still moving: "OMG!! You're still going!" Yes I was. I smiled to myself, not only at the message and what I had already achieved, but because for the first time since leaving Winchester I absolutely knew I was going to finish.

The climb out of Southease would be shit on a good day, but after having been on the move now for almost 24 hours it was quite frankly disgusting. From pretty close to sea level I slowly hiked my way up 700 feet to the peak over less than four miles. It took me an hour and a half to reach the top, but it was a summit that took me closer to the end. I could almost smell the finish. If I had my glasses on I might have even been able to see it. Dropping back down the other side of the hill I picked up my pace again conscious of the creeping time. My only concern now was the clock. I knew I had it in me to finish the distance, but if I slowed down too much, the cut-offs would start to get tighter and I really didn't have too much time to play with.

Ahead of me in the distance lay the picturesque village of Alfriston. It looked like the kind of place where people with money lived. With its pretty church and Tudor pubs it wouldn't be out of place as the backdrop of a television period drama. To me it was beautiful for only one reason though: as the penultimate checkpoint. Running into town, all that was going through my head was the song *Galveston* by Glenn Campbell, only with the place name exchanged. In my tired brain it sounded like a good replacement lyric and I sang the chorus on a loop as I made my way to the aid station. I was at 91.5 miles at 7:46am. I had made up some time over the last section and was feeling good. Telling the marshal my number I asked them to just re-fill my bottles. I wasn't stopping here. I was going to Eastbourne.

Much the same as leaving Southease, the first half of the journey to the final checkpoint at Jevington was uphill. Also like the previous climb it was long and slow going. But with only four miles to go to get there I was in the zone. Head down, again I hiked my way up the winding path to the top of the hill. The weather had started to turn and at the peak the wind was blustery and determined in its attempts to hold me up. After everything I'd already been through, a bit of wind wasn't going to stop me now. I was possessed by the desire to be able to stop but only after having finished. Across the top and then dropping down the other side towards the checkpoint, I started to catch and overtake other runners. Everyone looked exhausted and battling their own personal demons. "Nearly there dude," and "Well done, keep it going" were soundbites I reeled out repeatedly as I passed people. I was shifting but not out of competitive spirit to be in front of them, just to see this through.

As I ran into Jevington I could see the checkpoint ahead of me. My watch was telling me I had covered almost 96 miles in just under 27 hours. Just four more miles to go. As I approached the marshal standing outside the village hall I made sure he had my number and told him I wasn't stopping. "You've only got four miles left and you've got three hours to do it in. That's 45 minutes a mile. I think you're going to be fine," he said. He was right. I had been focussing so much on keeping inside the cut-off times I hadn't once flipped it around and thought about how long I had left to get to the finish. With no more checkpoints to have cut-offs on, the monster of being timed out disappeared before my very eyes.

I laughed to myself as I turned off the Jevington Road and back onto the South Downs Way. As I started my hike up the final hill the skies opened and the rain came. In complete contrast to the previous day where the heat had been the problem, now it was pissing down. But it didn't matter one bit. I stopped halfway up the hill and got my jacket out of my vest and put it on. It was a kind of fruitless task really as I was already soaked but it was more about keeping the wind from blowing through me.

As the foliage parted at the brow of the hill I saw a solitary volunteer standing next to trig point in the rain. His job was to make sure we didn't get lost now. That would be heart-breaking. Down below me Eastbourne was laid out like a map. It was a beautiful sight to behold. I'd been there before but I don't remember it looking this fantastic. "You see that big white building there," said the marshal pointing into the near distance, "that's the finish. You've got this! Down that gully to the left." I felt like crying.

I headed off down the rocky overgrown gully towards the sports ground. On the way downhill I passed a few more people who looked like they were in various states of pain. But they were all still moving. It was impossible to know from looking at them how the journey had been for them. Although we had all left Winchester the day before and were now at the other end of the South Downs Way, what had happened along the way and how it affected us would be unique and personal. I gave them words of encouragement as I went by and pushed on. As I made my way out onto the road, I left the shelter of the woods behind and the rain seemed heavier. I was soaked through but oblivious to any of it. The only thing in my focus now was finishing.

It was 9:50am on a Sunday morning in June and I was slowly running along King's Drive in Eastbourne, which most weekends would no doubt form part of a regular route for many a local runner. This morning however, as the heavy rain streamed the sweat into my eyes, I appeared to be on my own.

Passing the hospital I kept running along the pavement looking around for some small sign that I'm done, anything telling me I could finally stop running, but nothing was apparent. Fluttering from a tree I spotted a familiar piece of red and white tape and took a couple of left turns, taking me behind the hospital. I was exhausted but ecstatic. Keeping my feet moving in any semblance of a running motion is an effort, I knew I was close, so I kept shuffling forwards. But as I rounded the corner, the long winding footpath ahead shattered my resolve and I resigned myself to a walk. With rain soaking my face and wipers moving across the car windscreens, it would be impossible for anyone driving past to be able to tell there were tears mixing into the raindrops on my cheeks. I was a very tired, very happy man.

Turning the final corner my destination loomed into view. I wiped the rain from the screen of my watch. Time was irrelevant at this point. I was well inside the cut-off and even factoring in a degree of inaccuracy I could see I only had half a mile left to go. The end was quite literally in sight.

Entering Eastbourne Sports Park I joined the wet track and splashed my way through the puddles around the final 300 metres.

Looking over at the inflatable archway on the other side of the track I saw Paul waiting for me. As I rounded the final bend, the sense of euphoric relief that rose up in me was incredible. I had done it. One-hundred miles. I crossed the line in 28 hours and five minutes. Finally I could stop. I collected my buckle and posed for my finisher's photograph. What an experience!

I walked over to Paul and we shook hands and had a warm man embrace. I hadn't seen him since the Washington checkpoint almost 50 miles earlier, which I always thought could only be a good thing. If he had dropped out, I would no doubt have bumped into him at one of the checkpoints. But no, he had finished too. His progress over the second half of the race hadn't been too dissimilar to my own, especially given the half an hour I spent at Washington. He finished in an amazing 27 hours and one minute. Robin, who I hadn't seen since Winchester, also finished. But given he had crossed the line in just over 23 hours, he was literally already at home in bed. Of course he was.

As Paul and I left the track to go inside the sport centre I noticed he was hobbling like a crap robot, whereas my legs were still fluid and working. I laughed at his total inability to operate his legs. He stopped shuffling and looked at me: "You fucking wait, mate. You just fucking wait."

STILL NOT BIONIC

21. We Are Strong

Sitting inside the sports centre with a hot dog and coffee I stared at the buckle resting on my leg. It was well-made, weighty and good looking. More than any of its material attributes though, it was what it meant that really mattered. It was a physical manifestation of 28 hours of sweat and tears. It was mental torment, elation and determination all rolled into one. It was a thing of beauty. It merited a photo being posted to Twitter: "Job done. 28:05. #SDW100 #wasntshit." Within minutes my phone had gone into meltdown again.

Looking around there were people sprawled everywhere in various states of consciousness. We were remnants of the destruction invoked by covering 100 miles on foot against the clock. Just across from me was a table of finishers' t-shirts. As I attempted to get up from my chair to collect mine, Paul's words from the finish line rang through my head. Twenty minutes of sitting still had rendered my legs inoperable. I couldn't lift or bend them and as such had to resort to shuffling over to the table. With the shirts folded neatly in piles, I smiled as I saw they were a lovely white rather than a cursed orange. I was keeping that one for best.

With an hour and a half to go until the coach turned up to take us back to Winchester, I decided it would probably be a good idea to take a shower. The only problem was, looking in my bag, I didn't bring any shower gel. Or a towel. Or any clean clothes. I laughed. I had been so focussed on what I needed to do before and during the race that I hadn't put any thought to afterwards. Hobbling into the changing room I loudly announced my lack of a towel and asked if anybody could lend me one. The silence that came back was pretty clear it wasn't the done thing. I would need to improvise. After taking a water only shower - which frankly did little to eradicate the accumulated odour of a day's worth of running - I dried myself off with the t-shirt I had planned on wearing home. Luckily I had a new white one to wear instead. Unfortunately I couldn't say the same about my socks and underwear. I figured nobody else on the coach would notice or care. I certainly didn't. As the coach pulled up outside, a group of us shuffled aboard ready for the long drive back to where we left our cars the day before. Dropping into the seat, I rested my head against the cold window and passed out, eventually waking somewhere close to Winchester. It was much quicker getting back from Eastbourne than it had been getting there.

Disembarking the coach after sitting still for so long was an event of pure comedy. After I had painfully made my own way down the short set of steps, I stopped to watch those behind me attempting the same. It took some time but it was worth waiting for. Paul and I shuffled over to where I had left my car, dropped our bags in the boot and set out on the drive back to Bristol. After a snooze on the coach I was feeling reasonably awake now. Certainly far more awake than I had been when I imagined a double decker bus on the trail some hours earlier. We drove slowly home, stopping briefly to hobble around a shop near Salisbury for funny looks and a sandwich. By the time I pulled up outside my front door a couple of hours later, my legs had stopped working again. I contemplated how best to get out of the car and decided the easiest way was to just open the door and roll out onto the pavement. It wasn't graceful but it was effective. I was home and the weekend was over.

There had naturally been ups and downs along the way, but six months of hard work had finally paid off. More than that, it placed a neat cap on the last 15 months: failing to finish in Gran Canaria, pulling out of the previous year's South Downs Way 100, the wobbles, doubts and fears, in fact the entire rollercoaster of issues that had seen me question and re-evaluate everything I was doing. It was closure.

The following morning, after a restless night's sleep thanks to sore legs, my wife took me out for an epic full English breakfast. I'm not sure if bacon, sausage, eggs, mushrooms, beans, fried bread, potatoes, tomatoes, black pudding and a mug of tea were recognised cures for battered legs but I was certainly willing to give them a try. I had taken Monday as a day's holiday from work, which allowed me to ease my way back into normality slowly. Returning to the office on Tuesday, I shared my war stories from the weekend and tried not to grimace too hard when taking the six flights of stairs to my desk. There is a lift in the building but I've never used it and I wasn't about to start now.

With my legs feeling surprisingly good by Thursday I went to my running club for a six-mile run. It was amazing. By Friday I was feeling almost normal again and walked to my local pub and drank more beer than was good for me. Who was this man? The reality of what had happened over the previous few days still hadn't really sunk in, and in part that was down to the fact that life simply carried on. What was the point in sitting around moaning about feeling sore and not getting on with things? I had learnt a lot about myself over that 100 mile course and I can honestly say it changed my perspective on everything. Not just running and what I was capable of, but about life in general.

The challenge of running such a long distance does make you question yourself frequently, and it forces you to face up to your own personal demons. But when you eventually reach the end one thing shines through: you realise that no matter how bad it gets, you can always keep pushing on and in the end it is always worth it. In so many ways it's a great metaphor for dealing with depression. If you stop to think of all the adversity you've already overcome in life, you'll realise you've already come through it. You are still here in spite of all of that. You are already strong enough. We are all strong enough if we give ourselves the chance.

Running is a great way of engaging with yourself and having that difficult conversation: proving to yourself that you are worth it. I'm not saying running is a cure for mental health issues because it's not. Depression is a personal battle and nothing can replace professional help for somebody suffering with it, but exercise can complement treatment and help make you feel good about yourself. Possibly even just allow you to feel *something*. Exercising with friends also provides a natural support network that should never be underestimated in its capability to help you through tough times. Good friends will always be there for you, no matter what.

Depression has the capability to rob you of all sense of feeling until you are numb to life. The beauty I found in ultrarunning was that it helped me experience life and exorcise those feelings of nothingness and hopelessness. That could be through the misery and pain of hiking up a mountain after many hours on your feet, or it could be the euphoric high of crossing a finish line. Both are perfect examples of feeling something rather than nothing. As much as I still love lying on the floor with my cat, I would much rather do that in addition to experiencing life than as a mechanism to avoid it.

I framed my South Downs Way race number together with my finisher's photo and it now hangs on the wall in my dining room. Every day as I sit at the table to eat a meal, I look at that picture and remember. I remember the hills, I remember the misery, I remember the finish, but more than anything I remember it is always worth it. Depression is a killer but it needn't be that way. If it doesn't end a life, it can still make one seem not worth living. That is when we all need to remember that it is always worth it. Regardless of what has gone before, create adventure, whatever that might be. Don't allow yourself to live a life under the shadows thrown by a dark past. Create a bright future and your demons will have nowhere to hide. Live a life.

Acknowledgements

When you look back over a span of years as I have done in this book, you realise so many people play a part in the story of your own life. We like to think we are the masters of our destiny but almost everything we do is influenced or facilitated by others. Whether they are friends, strangers or even professional individuals just doing their job, everyone we meet has some impact on our lives. Over the course of this story, lots of amazing people have - sometimes inadvertently - helped make the events over the previous pages a reality. For that I would like to thank them enormously.

Undoubtedly the single person who has played such an instrumental part in the events of the past three years has been Paul Wootten. Without Paul I would often have had nobody to go on my madcap adventures with. Together we have been through valleys and mountains, days and nights, misery and joy. It's been a blast and I'm sure it's still only the beginning.

For all the individuals who read the very rough edits and first drafts I churned out to gauge feedback on ideas for this book, I would like to thank you. In particular Jim Smith, Kate Allen, Andy Hulcoop and Bear Schlenker. The conversations between us have driven ideas, reshaped chapters and helped form the book you have just read. I would especially like to thank Jane Duffus for her critical analysis on the content as much as the grammar and punctuation. Being so engrossed in a story means you often end up working from a state of assumed knowledge, and her grounding of the story in the real world helped define the clarity of the end product. Likewise, without the amazing help and support of Richard Jones at Tangent Books, who puts up with my constant badgering, you wouldn't even be holding this book now.

My GP Dr Richard Berkley once again proved to be the most patient, understanding and persistent of doctors on the planet. His help through my period of depression was amazing. His constant quest to drill down into the unanswered questions saw me ending up having more tests and meetings with consultants than my National Insurance contributions could surely ever fund. For his tenacity I am eternally grateful. I would also like to extend a huge thank you to LIFT, the mental health support service which was instrumental in my rehabilitation. Talking to them, especially initially, was such a difficult thing to do but if I hadn't I would now be in a very different place.

A special thank you has to go out to every single person who read *Fat Man to Green Man* and then got in touch to tell me how much they enjoyed it, and in some cases how it changed lives. I can't tell you how humbling it is to receive such feedback. When you sit at a computer for months at a time, trying to write out things you've been through in a creative, entertaining and informative way, it is so easy to lose sight of what you're creating and why you started it. I am still constantly amazed by how that book is received and if this book even touches a fraction of the success that has then I'll be extremely happy.

Running 100 miles was a serious undertaking that has reframed everything I thought possible. While I made it to the finish, it absolutely wouldn't have been possible without the slick organisation of James and Nici at Centurion Running and the incredible army of volunteers who staffed the checkpoints, re-filled my bottles and kept me fed and motivated. The unquestioning support from friends, acquaintances and total strangers alike is an incredible element to running ultra events and constantly surprising in its depth and honesty.

I would like to say a special thank you to everyone who has allowed me so kindly to use their photographs in this book - Steve Worrallo, Annemarie Hoskins, Carol Aleknavicius, Bridget White, Stuart March (Stuart March Photography), Andrew Rendell and Brandon Griffiths (AWOL Adventure). The images really help add to the story.

Finally, but undeniably the biggest and most important thank you - once again - must go to my wife and family who over the years have constantly tolerated the crazy ideas I have come up with, nursed me when I've been down, supported me and given me the freedom to undertake the adventures that have coloured my life. Without them this story would never have begun.

If you would like to get in touch to let me know your thoughts on this book you can find me on Twitter. I am on Facebook as well, but to be honest I never look at it. Who has the time for multiple social media channels?

Web: https://twitter.com/IraRainey

The South Downs Way 100 is organised by Centurion Running. They organise ultra distance trail events around the south of the UK and are backed up by an incredible team of volunteers.

Web: http://www.centurionrunning.com

The Green Man Ultra and Green Man Midnight Express are both organised by Ultra Running. They put on lots of other ultramarathons all over the UK.

Web: http://www.ultrarunning.uk.com

If you feel like you could be experiencing mental health issues then do not ignore those feelings. It is nothing to ashamed of and people are there for you and to help you. Things are not hopeless and you are never truly alone. Please reach out and talk to somebody, anybody. Whether that is a confidential helpline or face-to-face with your own GP, people will listen. Here are some great starting points:

Every 90 seconds someone in the UK or Ireland dies by suicide, but you don't need to be suicidal to ask for help. The Samaritans are there to listen to you - 24 hours a day, 365 days a year. You can call them for free from any phone at any time of the day. Don't suffer alone and don't dismiss your own misery. Talking helps.

Phone: 116 123
Web: http://www.samaritans.org

Mind is a mental health charity which provides advice and support to empower anyone experiencing a mental health problem. They campaign to improve services, raise awareness and promote understanding. Whether you are experiencing issues or are just interested in finding out more, they can help you.

Phone: 0300 123 3393
Web: http://www.mind.org.uk

Macmillan Cancer Support provides practical, medical, emotional and financial support to those suffering from cancer and those who support them. We are all affected by cancer, so why not take the money you would normally spend on treating yourself from just one night of the month and give it to help somebody who needs it more instead?

Phone: 0808 808 00 00
Web: http://www.macmillan.org.uk